Better Homes and (

WOODWORKING
PROJECTS
COUNTRY-STYLE

MURDOCH BOOKS®

Sydney • London • Vancouver • New York

Contents

Masterpiece in Pine

This smart pine cabinet can be used as either a home entertainment unit or as a traditional wardrobe for the bedroom. Whatever role it performs, it will do it with style.

CONSTRUCTING THE SIDE PANELS

1 Edge-join timber to form the cabinet sides (A), bottom (B) and top (C) to the sizes shown in the Timber list on page 5 but with an extra 13 mm in width and 25 mm in length.

2 Lay out the panels and choose the best grain match. Mark the edges that will receive the splines (see the Cabinet Assembly diagram and Spline Detail diagram, page 6).

3 Using a 6 mm slotting cutter, rout 6 mm slots, centred, along the marked edges of the panels. Stop the slots 51 mm from the ends for the top panel (C) but rout the side and bottom panels the full length of the timber. Refer to the Spline Detail diagram on the Cabinet Assembly diagram (page 6).

4 From 6 mm plywood, cut 23 mm wide splines to the lengths needed to fit the routed slots. Cut or sand the ends of the top panel splines to shape.

5 Glue, spline and clamp the side panels (A), bottom panel (B) and top panel (C) together, checking that the panels remain flat. Remove excess adhesive.

6 Rip and crosscut the panels (A, B, C) to the finished sizes shown in the Timber list on page 5.

7 Measuring 64 mm from the front and back edges of the side panels, cut a pair of 13 mm deep grooves, 18 mm wide plus an extra 2 mm for clearance, for the shelf strippings.

ASSEMBLING THE CABINET

8 From 19 mm pine, rip and crosscut a piece 137 x 915 mm long for the bottom front rail (D), and a piece 101 x 915 mm long for top front rail (E).

Adjustable shelves make this handsome pine cabinet versatile enough to fulfil a number of storage requirements.

TIMBER

PART	FINISHED SIZE IN MM			MATERIAL	QUANTITY
	W	T	L		
CABINET					
A* sides	537	19	1378	EP	2
B* bottom	537	19	876	EP	1
C* top	632	19	1067	EP	1
D bottom rail	137	19	914	P	1
E top rail	101	19	914	P	1
F cleats	25	19	537	P	2
G cleats	25	19	508	P	2
H cleats	25	19	838	P	3
I back	895	6	1242	H	1
MOULDING					
J* bottom side	133	19	575	P	2
K* bottom front	133	19	952	P	1
L* bottom sides	117	19	593	P	2
M* bottom front	117	19	490	P	1
N top sides	70	19	575	P	2
O top front	70	19	953	P	1
P* dentil mould	25	13	568	P	2
Q* dentil mould	25	13	940	P	1
R* crown mould	64	47	622	P	2
S* crown mould	64	47	1048	P	1
DOORS					
T stiles	64	19	1137	P	4
U top rails	64	19	356	P	2
V bottom rails	96	19	356	P	2
W* panels	352	19	1002	EP	2
SHELVES					
X* shelves	457	19	873	EP	3
Y* fronts	38	19	873	P	3

Initially, cut parts marked with an * oversized. Then, trim each to finished size according to the step-by-step instructions.

Material key: EP = edge-joined pine, P = pine, H = hardboard

OTHER MATERIALS

- 13 x 6 g flathead wood screws
- 20 x 6 g flathead wood screws
- 32 x 8 g flathead wood screws
- 2400 mm pine crown moulding
- Three pairs of pivot hinges
- Two pulls
- Four roller catches
- Four 16 mm brown or walnut finished shelf strippings
- Four 150 mm shelf supports (to suit stripping)
- Six brackets
- 6 mm plywood
- Woodworking adhesive
- Wood conditioner; stain; clear finish

9 From 25 x 19 mm thick pine, cut two pieces 537 mm long, a piece 508 mm long and a piece 838 mm long, for the cleats (F, G, H). Drill and countersink the mounting holes through the cleats.

10 Position and square the side cleats (F) on the cabinet sides (A) (see the Cabinet Assembly diagram, page 6). Screw the cleats in place. Then position and screw the top cleats (G) in place.

TOOLS

- Table saw
- Hack saw
- Router
- Router bits: 6 mm slotting cutter, 10 mm slotting cutter, 6 mm ovalo cutter
- Drill
- Drill bits: 2.5 mm, 3.5 mm, countersink
- Builder's square
- 13 mm chisel
- 40 mm hole saw (optional)
- Wooden mitre gauge (crosscut fence)
- Dado blade
- Orbital sander

Substitute other tools or equipment as desired. Additional common hand tools and clamps may be required when completing this project.

Always observe the safety precautions outlined in the owner's manual when using a tool or a piece of machinery.

11 Dry-clamp the bottom and top panels (B, C) to the side panels with their back edges flush with the back edges of the sides. The top panel should overhang both side panels by 76 mm. Check for square and screw but do not glue the panels together.

12 Dry-clamp the rails (D, E) in place, drill countersunk screw holes and glue and screw the rails to the unit.

13 Rout a 10 mm rebate 6 mm deep along the back inside edge of the assembled cabinet. Chisel each of the corners square.

14 Measure the rebated opening and cut the back (I) to size from 6 mm hardboard. If you plan to use the cabinet for electronic components, bore ventilation and wire access holes (see the Cabinet Assembly diagram, page 6).

ADDING THE PINE MOULDING

15 Cut the bottom trim pieces (J, K, L, M) to size plus 25 mm in length (see the Timber list, above).

16 Referring to the Exploded View diagram (page 9) and the Lower Moulding Detail diagram (page 8), rout a 13 mm cove along the top front edge of the

CUTTING

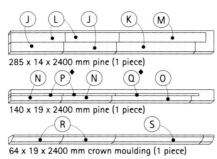

285 x 14 x 2400 mm pine (2 pieces)

285 x 19 x 2400 mm pine (1 piece)

285 x 19 x 2400 mm pine (1 piece)

185 x 19 x 2400 mm pine (2 pieces)

285 x 14 x 2400 mm pine (1 piece)

140 x 19 x 2400 mm pine (1 piece)

64 x 19 x 2400 mm crown moulding (1 piece)

◆ Plane or resaw to thickness stated in Timber list

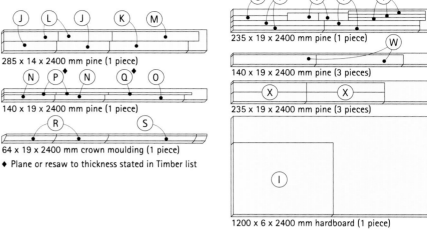

235 x 19 x 2400 mm pine (1 piece)

140 x 19 x 2400 mm pine (3 pieces)

235 x 19 x 2400 mm pine (3 pieces)

1200 x 6 x 2400 mm hardboard (1 piece)

SPLINE DETAIL

Length of spline equals spline slot length minus 3 mm

Timber to be joined

6 mm slots 13 mm deep centered on edge

6 mm spline 23 mm wide

51 mm

51 mm

Shape end of spline to fit groove

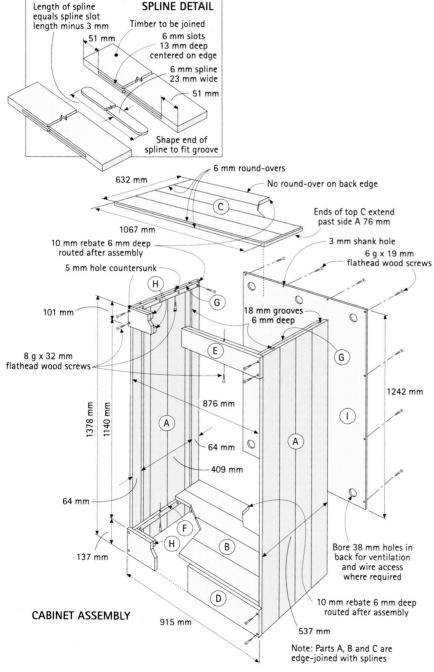

CABINET ASSEMBLY

6 mm round-overs

No round-over on back edge

632 mm

1067 mm

Ends of top C extend past side A 76 mm

3 mm shank hole

6 g x 19 mm flathead wood screws

10 mm rebate 6 mm deep routed after assembly

5 mm hole countersunk

18 mm grooves 6 mm deep

101 mm

8 g x 32 mm flathead wood screws

1378 mm

1140 mm

876 mm

1242 mm

64 mm

409 mm

64 mm

137 mm

Bore 38 mm holes in back for ventilation and wire access where required

10 mm rebate 6 mm deep routed after assembly

915 mm

537 mm

Note: Parts A, B and C are edge-joined with splines

inner trim pieces (J, K). Mitre-cut the pieces and screw but do not glue them to the bottom of the cabinet.

17 Rout a 13 mm bead along the top front edge of the moulding pieces (L, M). Mitre-cut these pieces and glue them to the cabinet.

18 Cut the top trim pieces (N, O) to size and screw but do not glue them to the top of the cabinet.

19 Cut dentil mould pieces (P, Q) to size plus an extra 57 mm in length. Referring to the Cutting the Dentil Mould diagram (page 7), construct the jig shown. (The centre of the 3 mm kerf in the mitre extension should be 13 mm from the centre of the indexing pin.) Make one kerfing cut across the end of one of the dentil mould strips. Then position this kerf on the indexing pin and make the second cut. Referring to the Step 19 illustration below, continue the process until you have made all the evenly spaced kerfs. Then repeat the process for each piece.

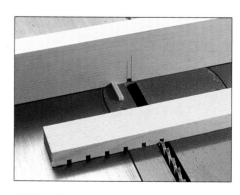

STEP 19 Use a wooden mitre-gauge (crosscut fence) extension with a guide for cutting the dentil mould.

RIPPING THE CROWN MOULDING

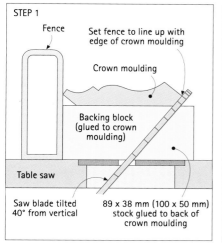

STEP 1

Fence

Set fence to line up with edge of crown moulding

Crown moulding

Backing block (glued to crown moulding)

Table saw

Saw blade tilted 40° from vertical

89 x 38 mm (100 x 50 mm) stock glued to back of crown moulding

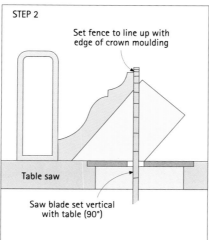

STEP 2

Set fence to line up with edge of crown moulding

Table saw

Saw blade set vertical with table (90°)

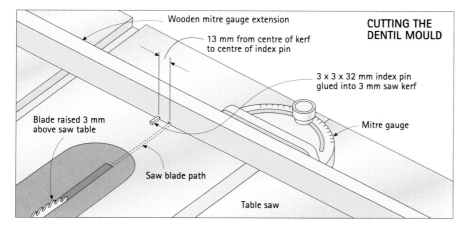

Wooden mitre gauge extension

13 mm from centre of kerf to centre of index pin

CUTTING THE DENTIL MOULD

3 x 3 x 32 mm index pin glued into 3 mm saw kerf

Mitre gauge

Blade raised 3 mm above saw table

Saw blade path

Table saw

20 Mitre-cut the dentil mould pieces (P, Q) and glue them to the cabinet where marked on the Exploded View diagram (page 9).

21 Select a straight, flat 100 x 50 mm piece of timber and glue it to the back face of a 2400 mm long piece of crown moulding purchased from a hardware store (see Step 1 of the Ripping the Crown Moulding diagram, above). Then rip the edges of the lamination where shown in Steps 1 and 2 of the Ripping the Crown Moulding diagram.

22 Measure and mitre-cut the front mould piece (S) to length and glue it to the top front of the cabinet. Repeat this procedure for the side mould pieces (R).

CONSTRUCTING A PAIR OF DOORS

23 Cut the door stiles (T), top rails (U), and bottom rails (V) to size (see the Timber list, page 5).

24 Attach a 2 mm dado blade to the table saw and raise it 13 mm above the surface of the saw table. Cut a 6 mm groove, centred from side to side, along one edge of each part (see the Door diagram and the Tenon Detail diagram on page 8). (To ensure that the groove is directly in the centre, test-cut it in a piece of scrap timber the same thickness as the stiles and rails.)

25 Using a mitre gauge (crosscut fence) with an attached wood extension for support, form the stub tenons by cutting a 13 mm rebate 6.5 mm deep on both faces of each end of the rails.

26 Edge-join narrower, straight-grained 19 mm pine to form two door panels (W) that measure 377 mm wide and 1027 mm long.

27 When the adhesive has dried completely, cut the door panels to finished size (see the Timber list, page 5).

28 Tilt your table saw blade 5 degrees from vertical and raise the blade 57 mm above the saw table. Position the rip fence, then test-cut scrap timber to create the shape shown on the Raised-panel Detail diagram on the Door diagram (page 8) and cut each edge of each panel. Sand the cut areas to remove saw marks.

29 Test-fit the door pieces and trim if necessary. Then finish-sand the panels and stain them. Glue and clamp each door, checking for square. Rest the clamped assemblies on a flat surface.

ADDING THE PIVOT HINGES

30 Mark the upper and lower hinge recesses where marked on the Top and Bottom Hinge Recess diagram (see page 8). Then mark the locations for the middle notches where shown on the Middle Hinge Notch diagram (see page 8). Following the instructions supplied with the pivot hinges, form the top, bottom and middle hinge recesses and notches.

31 Mount the hinges to the doors and fasten the hinges to the cabinet. Mount the roller catches to the doors and cabinet.

32 Drill the holes for the pulls. Attach the pulls and catches. Install the shelf strippings in the cabinet.

CONSTRUCTING THE SHELVES

33 Using the procedure listed above to form the panels for the side, bottom and top panels, edge-join and spline enough pine timber for the number of shelves (X) required (see the Timber list, page 5). (Note that to allow electrical cords passage to the wire-access holes, there is a gap of 25 mm between the back edge of the shelf and the front edge of the back piece (I).) Cut the shelves to fit between the shelf strippings.

34 Cut the shelf fronts (Y) to size plus 25 mm in length (see Timber list, page 5). Referring to the Shelf Detail diagram on the Shelf diagram (see page 9), cut a 19 mm rebate 6 mm deep along the back edge of each. Glue and clamp a front to each shelf.

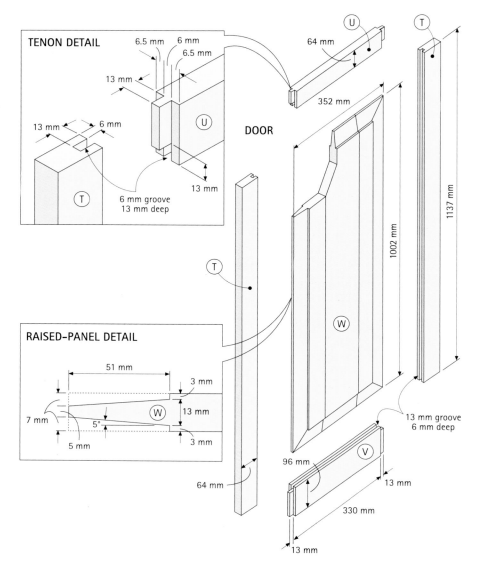

TENON DETAIL

6.5 mm
6 mm
6.5 mm
13 mm
13 mm
6 mm
13 mm
U
T
6 mm groove
13 mm deep

DOOR

U
64 mm
T
352 mm
1137 mm
1002 mm
T
W
13 mm groove
6 mm deep

RAISED-PANEL DETAIL

51 mm
3 mm
7 mm
13 mm
5°
W
5 mm
3 mm

64 mm

96 mm
V
13 mm
330 mm
13 mm

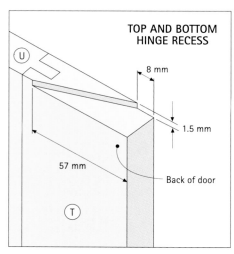

TOP AND BOTTOM HINGE RECESS

U
8 mm
1.5 mm
57 mm
Back of door
T

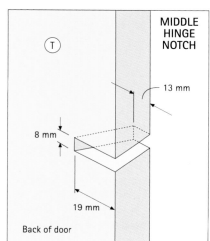

MIDDLE HINGE NOTCH

T
13 mm
8 mm
19 mm
Back of door

35 Rout 6 mm beads along the front edge of each shelf front. Trim the ends of the shelf fronts flush with the ends of each shelf.

36 Fit the shelf support brackets onto the stripping and check the fit of your shelves. They should slip in with about 2 mm clearance and sit flat on the shelf supports.

37 Carefully remove each piece of hardware from the cabinet. Take off the hardware from each of the cabinet doors. Remove the back (I) from the cabinet. Finish-sand all the pieces of the cabinet. Then apply the finish of your choice.

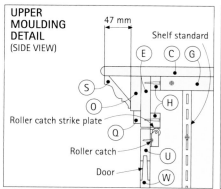

UPPER MOULDING DETAIL
(SIDE VIEW)

47 mm
Shelf standard
E   C   G
S
O
H
Roller catch strike plate
Q
Roller catch
U
Door
W

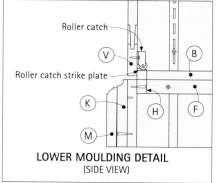

Roller catch
V
B
Roller catch strike plate
K
H
F
M

LOWER MOULDING DETAIL
(SIDE VIEW)

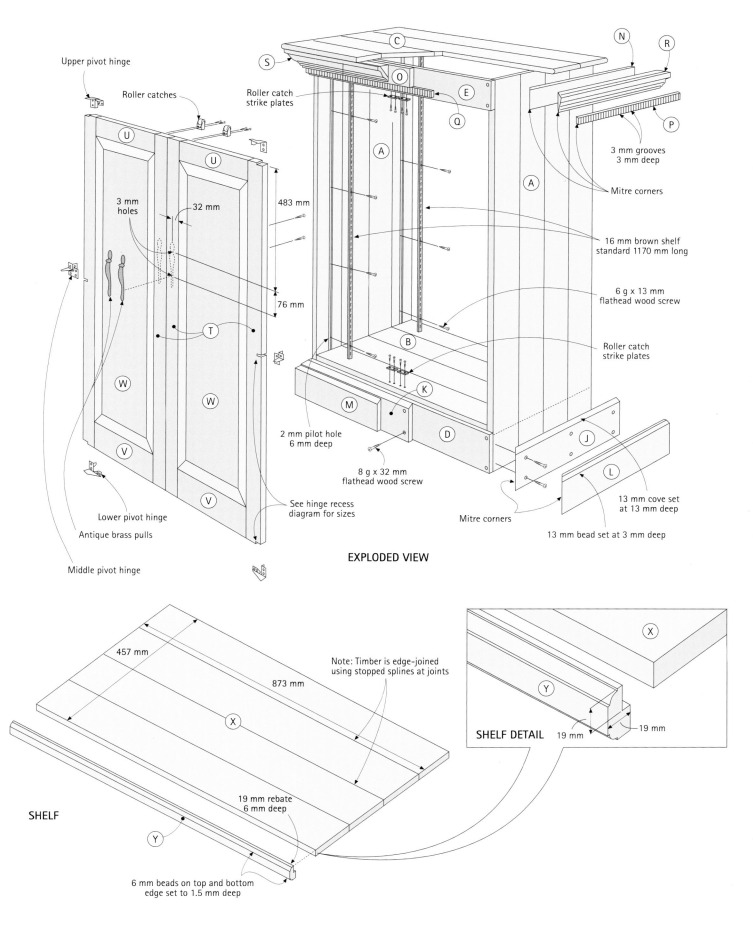

Upper pivot hinge

Roller catches

Roller catch
strike plates

3 mm
holes

32 mm

483 mm

76 mm

Lower pivot hinge

Antique brass pulls

Middle pivot hinge

See hinge recess
diagram for sizes

EXPLODED VIEW

3 mm grooves
3 mm deep

Mitre corners

16 mm brown shelf
standard 1170 mm long

6 g x 13 mm
flathead wood screw

Roller catch
strike plates

2 mm pilot hole
6 mm deep

8 g x 32 mm
flathead wood screw

Mitre corners

13 mm cove set
at 13 mm deep

13 mm bead set at 3 mm deep

457 mm

873 mm

Note: Timber is edge-joined
using stopped splines at joints

SHELF DETAIL   19 mm

19 mm

SHELF

19 mm rebate
6 mm deep

6 mm beads on top and bottom
edge set to 1.5 mm deep

Early Days Sofa Table

Standing behind a sofa or in a hallway, this elegant, practical table
with its single drawer, painted base and stained top will draw rave reviews.

CONSTRUCTING THE LEGS

1 Cut eight pieces of 41 x 19 mm thick pine, 768 mm long. With the edges and ends flush, glue and clamp together two pieces of pine, face to face, for each leg (A).

2 Scrape the excess adhesive from one edge of each leg and joint or plane the scraped edge. Using a table saw, rip the opposite edge of each leg for a finished width of 38 mm. Trim both ends of each leg for a 743 mm finished length.

3 Referring to the Leg Blank diagram (see page 11), mark the centre points. Then, using a dowelling jig, drill 10 mm holes, 16 mm deep on two adjoining sides of each leg (see the Leg Blank diagram). Mark the cut lines on all four surfaces of one leg.

4 Following the sequence of steps on the Cutting the Tapers diagram (page 12), taper-cut the four legs to shape.

ADDING THE RAILS

5 From 19 mm pine, cut two pieces 140 x 176 mm long for the side rails (B), and a piece 140 x 812 mm long for the back rail (C).

6 Cut the front rail parts (D) to the sizes shown on the Front Rail diagram (page 12). Referring to the Step 6 illustration below, glue and clamp the front rail, making sure the ends are flush.

7 To form the pattern for the front rail, lay out the Half-pattern for Front diagram (page 12) on a piece of heavy paper 507 x 50 mm. To do this, draw a 25 mm grid on the piece of paper and using the grid pattern for reference, mark the points where the pattern outline crosses each grid line, then draw lines to connect the points. Cut along the outline of the pattern, position the bottom of the template flush with the bottom of the front rail and use it to lay out the curved bottom on one half of the rail. Flip the pattern over (so that you have the mirror image) and mark the outline on the other half of the rail.

JOINING THE RAILS TO THE LEGS

8 Using dowel centres, transfer the dowel-hole centre points from the legs to the side rails (B), back rail (C), and front rail (D). The rails are set back 10 mm from the face of the legs (see the Corner Detail diagram on the Exploded View diagram, page 13).

9 Referring to the Exploded View diagram (see page 13), drill 10 mm holes 23 mm deep in the ends of the rails for the dowel pins.

10 Glue and clamp a side rail between a front and rear leg. Repeat this process, using the other side rail and the remaining front and rear legs.

11 Referring to the Step 11 illustration (right), glue the back rail (C) and front rail (D) between the leg assemblies. Check for square and twist.

The table's simple lines are enlivened by decorative curved edges on the front rail.

STEP 6 Check that the ends are flush when clamping the front rail pieces.

TIMBER

PART	FINISHED SIZE IN MM			MATERIAL	QUANTITY
	W	T	L		
TABLE					
A* legs	38	38	743	LP	4
B sides	140	19	178	P	2
C back	140	19	812	P	1
D front	140	19	812	EP	1
E cleats	19	19	150	P	2
F drawer liners	114	19	197	P	2
G guides	19	19	197	P	4
H cleats	19	19	114	P	4
I* top	267	19	915	EP	1
DRAWER					
J sides	67	13	213	P	2
K front	67	13	368	P	1
L back	51	13	368	P	1
M bottom	156	6	368	PW	1
N face	92	19	406	P	1

*Initially cut parts marked with an * oversized, then trim each to the finished size according to the step-by step instructions.

Material key: P = pine, LP = laminated pine, EP = edge-joined pine, PW = plywood

OTHER MATERIALS

- 25 mm diameter knob
- 8 g x 30 mm round head brass wood screw
- 11 x 38 mm dowel pins
- 8 g x 25 mm flathead wood screws; 10 g x 32 mm roundhead wood screws
- Woodworking adhesive
- 5 mm washers
- 25 mm brads
- Double-faced (carpet) tape
- Finish

TOOLS

- Table saw
- Dado blade or dado set
- Band saw
- Jointer
- Drill
- Drill bits: 3 mm, 3.5 mm, 10 mm
- Router
- Router bits: 10 mm round-over, 13 mm round-over
- Orbital sander

Substitute other tools or equipment as desired. Additional common hand tools and clamps may be required.

Always observe the safety precautions in the owner's manual when using a tool or piece of machinery.

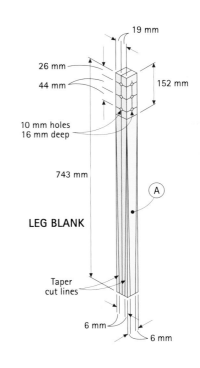

19 mm
26 mm
44 mm
152 mm
10 mm holes
16 mm deep
743 mm

LEG BLANK

A

Taper cut lines

6 mm

6 mm

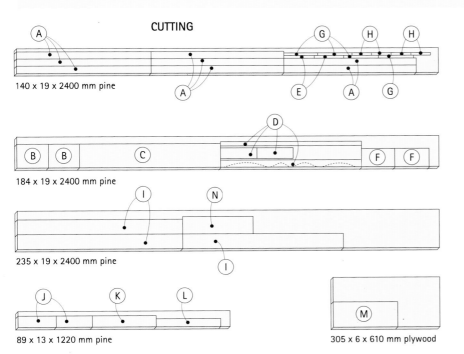

CUTTING

A   A   G   H   H

A   E   A   G

140 x 19 x 2400 mm pine

D

B   B   C   F   F

184 x 19 x 2400 mm pine

I   N

235 x 19 x 2400 mm pine   I

J   K   L

89 x 13 x 1220 mm pine

M

305 x 6 x 610 mm plywood

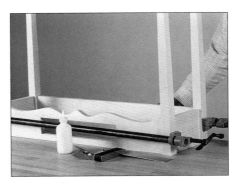

STEP 11   Clamp the front rail and back rail between the leg assemblies.

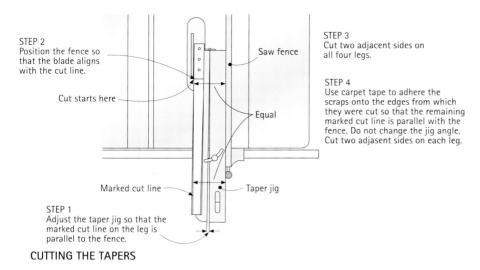

STEP 2
Position the fence so that the blade aligns with the cut line.

Cut starts here

Saw fence

Equal

STEP 3
Cut two adjacent sides on all four legs.

STEP 4
Use carpet tape to adhere the scraps onto the edges from which they were cut so that the remaining marked cut line is parallel with the fence. Do not change the jig angle. Cut two adjasent sides on each leg.

Marked cut line

Taper jig

STEP 1
Adjust the taper jig so that the marked cut line on the leg is parallel to the fence.

CUTTING THE TAPERS

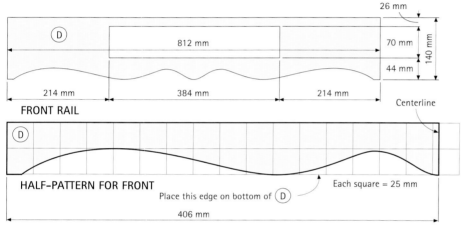

26 mm

D

812 mm

70 mm

140 mm

44 mm

214 mm

384 mm

214 mm

FRONT RAIL

Centerline

D

HALF-PATTERN FOR FRONT

Place this edge on bottom of D

Each square = 25 mm

406 mm

12 From 19 mm pine, cut two pieces 19 x 150 mm long, for the cleats (E). Then, referring to Corner Detail diagram on the Exploded View diagram (see page 13), drill the mounting holes. (Drill one of the top mounting holes a little oversized so that the screw can move slightly as the top of the table expands and contracts.) Glue and screw the cleats to the inside edges of the side rails.

INSTALLING THE DRAWER GUIDES

13 With a tape measure, check the distance between the front piece (D) and back piece (C), then cut the drawer liners (F) and guides (G) to the sizes shown in the Timber list (page 11) and to the measured length.

14 Glue and nail the guides in position (see the Exploded View diagram, page 13). Make sure that they are flush with the top and bottom edges of the drawer opening.

15 Cut the mounting cleats (H) to size and glue and nail them flush with the ends of the outside surface of each drawer liner.

16 Glue and nail the drawer-guide assemblies (F, G, H) between the front and back rails, making sure the inside edge of the drawer liners (F) is flush with the inside edge of the drawer opening in the front rail.

CONSTRUCTING THE TABLETOP

17 Cut three pieces of 89 x 19 mm thick pine, 940 mm long for the top panel (I). Edge-join the pieces of pine, making sure the surfaces and ends are flush. Use clamp blocks between the clamps and the wood pieces to prevent denting the pine edges.

18 Remove the excess glue and sand smooth. Trim the top panel to 915 mm long. Referring to the Edge Detail

diagram on the Exploded View diagram (page 13), rout a 6 mm round-over bit along the front and side edges of the tabletop.

ADDING THE DRAWER

19 Rip and crosscut the drawer sides (J), front (K), back (L) and bottom (M) (see the Timber list, page 11).

20 Cut a 6 mm groove 10 mm deep in the bottom edge of the drawer sides and drawer front (see the Drawer diagram, page 13). Then cut a 13 mm trench 6 mm deep, 51 mm from the back end of each drawer side. Cut a 13 mm rebate 6 mm deep along the front inside edge of each drawer side.

21 Referring to the Drawer diagram (page 13), drill and countersink a pair of 3.5 mm holes through the drawer front (K) for the drawer face (N).

22 Dry-clamp the drawer pieces to check their fit and to check the fit of the drawer in the front opening. Then glue and clamp the drawer together, checking for square. (To catch excess adhesive, preventing you from needing to remove it later, butt masking tape on the inside of each drawer corner. When the adhesive has dried, peel off the tape.) Do not glue the bottom (M) in the 6 mm groove. Instead, secure it to the back (L) with 25 mm brads.

23 Cut the drawer face (N) to size. Drill a 3 mm hole in the centre of the face for attaching the knob.

24 With the router, rout a 10 mm round-over along the front edges of the drawer face.

25 Screw the drawer face (N) to the drawer front (K).

FINISHING

26 Sand smooth the base, tabletop and drawer and apply a finish of your choice. For information on how to achieve the painted antique finish on the table base photographed, refer to the techniques described in the colonial candle box project (see page 107). A walnut stain, clear lacquer, cajun red paint, soldier blue paint, mahogany gel stain and satin polyurethane were applied

to the table base for this project. The tabletop was given a natural, aged wood finish. To achieve this look, the tabletop must first be distressed by scratching and denting the parts that would have received the greatest wear over the years, then a number of finishes applied. Follow the detailed instructions in the punched-tin pie safe project (see page 75). A traditional walnut stain was used for the tabletop here, followed by a jet mahogany gel stain, splattered on with toothbrush, then two coats of clear satin polyurethane.

27 When the finish has dried, place the tabletop (I) upside down on a blanket on your workbench. Turn the table base upside down also and position it on the tabletop. With the back edges flush, centre the base from side to side. Referring to the Exploded View diagram, screw the base to the top through the mounting cleats (E). Insert the roundhead wood screws with washers through the 10 mm holes and drive them in tightly. Then loosen the screws one full turn to allow for seasonal expansions and contractions of the top.

28 Add a 25 mm knob to the drawer. A porcelain knob attached with a 32 x 8 g round head brass wood screw was used for the drawer. To prevent the screw from working loose, add a drop of epoxy to the threads.

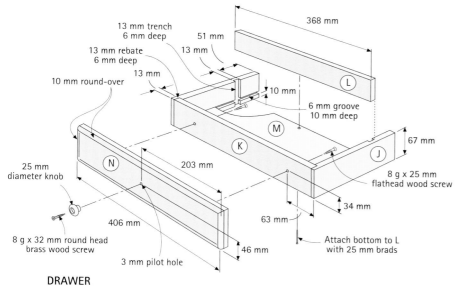

DRAWER

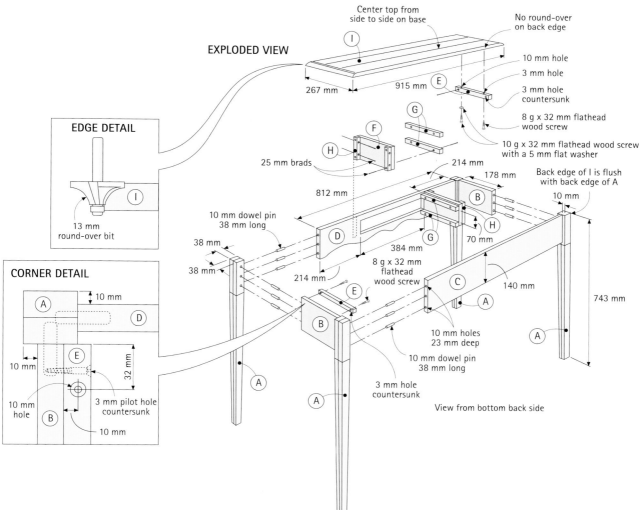

EXPLODED VIEW

EDGE DETAIL

CORNER DETAIL

Comfy Country Chair

This affordable, easy-to-build chair is part of a duo of comfortable outdoor furniture. It's stylish enough to occupy its own place in your favourite outdoor area, or you could make it to accompany the Comfy Country Bench.

BUILDING THE CHAIR ENDS

1 From 38 mm or edge-joined timber, cut the ends (A) to size (see Timber list, page 15).

2 Increase the Heart Half-pattern (see page 17) by 200 per cent, and transfer it onto a piece of heavy paper or poster board and cut to shape.

3 Referring to the End View diagram (page 16), position the template and trace the half-heart outline on all four end pieces (A). Cut the marked outlines to shape on the band saw or with a jigsaw and drum-sand the cut edges to remove the saw marks.

4 Clamp each matching pair of 285 x 38 mm ends together, heart edge to edge. Make sure that the top and bottom edges are flush.

5 Referring to the Exploded View diagram (see page 17), mark the two dowel-hole locations on one face. Remove the clamps. Using a square, transfer the lines to the inside edge of each end piece.

6 Using an electric drill and a Forstner bit, bore 19 mm holes 38 mm deep centred from edge to edge where marked. (Make sure that the holes are drilled square to the edge.)

7 Set a stop and cross-cut four pieces of 19 mm oak dowel timber to 86 mm long. Use a belt sander to sand a chamfer on each end of the dowels so that they are easy to insert.

8 From leftover timber, cut four 10 mm thick spacers. Glue, dowel and clamp both chair ends together, positioning the 10 mm spacers between the end pieces (A) so that the gap between the pieces on both chair ends is consistent. Save the spacers for joining the seat and the back pieces together later.

Made from durable timber such as dry oregon, the chair is built for the outdoors.

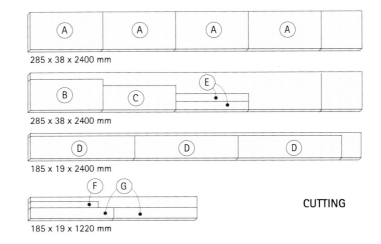

285 x 38 x 2400 mm

285 x 38 x 2400 mm

185 x 19 x 2400 mm

185 x 19 x 1220 mm

CUTTING

TOOLS

- Table saw
- Band saw or jigsaw
- Portable electric drill
- Drill bits: 10 mm
- Forstner bit: 19 mm
- Drum sander
- Router
- Router bits: 13 mm round-over
- 10 mm plug cutter
- Trammel points
- Orbital sander

Always observe the safety precautions in the owner's manual when using a tool or a piece of machinery.

TIMBER

PART	FINISHED SIZE IN MM			MATERIAL	QUANTITY
	W	T	L		
A ends	285	38	527	O	4
B seat front	235	38	533	O	1
C seat rear	185	38	533	O	1
D splats	171	19	762	O	3
E cleats	64	38	533	O	2
F cleat	38	19	495	O	1
G armrests	76	19	610	O	2

Material key: O = dry (seasoned) oregon, fir, treated pine* or redwood

In the absence of straight, uncupped timber, edge-join narrower pieces to width.

* When using treated pine, care must be taken to avoid inhaling dust. Consult your supplier for information regarding safety precautions.

OTHER MATERIALS

- Two 19 x 910 mm lengths of oak dowel
- 8 g x 30 mm deck screws
- 8 g x 50 mm deck screws
- Primer, exterior-grade stain or paint
- Water-resistant adhesive, slow-set epoxy or resorcinol adhesive

9 Referring to the End View diagram (see page 16), use trammel points to swing an arc to mark the 390 mm radius on the bottom end of each chair assembly. Cut the arcs to shape. Using a router, sand a slight round-over on all edges of each chair end assembly.

CONSTRUCTING THE SEAT

10 From 38 mm dry oregon, cut a piece 235 x 533 mm long for the seat front (B) and a piece 185 x 533 mm long for the seat rear (C). (You could rip the pieces to width from 300 x 50 mm timber.)

11 With the router, rout a 13 mm round-over along the top front edge of the seat front piece (B).

BUILDING THE BACKREST

12 From 19 mm dry oregon, cut three 172 x 762 mm long pieces for the backrest splats (D). Cut two pieces of 38 mm dry oregon 64 x 533 mm long and a piece of 19 mm dry oregon 38 x 495 mm long for the cleats (E, F).

13 Referring to the Chair Back diagram (see page 16), mark a 152 mm radius on two of the backrest splats. Cut the corners to shape and sand smooth to remove the saw marks.

14 To keep the back edge of the middle cleat (E) flush with the back edges of both the ends (A), bevel-rip a 25 degrees chamfer along the cleat's top edge (see the End View diagram, page 16).

15 Referring to the Chair Back and Exploded View diagrams (see pages 16 and 17), clamp the cleats (E, F) against the splats (D), using the 10 mm spacers to create gaps between the splats. Check for square.

DRILLING THE DOWEL HOLES

16 Referring to the End View diagram (see page 16), on the outside face of each seat end assembly mark the seat centreline then the centreline for the backrest cleats. Locate and mark the six dowel-hole centre points on the marked lines on each chair end.

17 Bore 19 mm holes through the chair ends at the marked centre points, backing the timber with scrap to prevent chip-out.

ASSEMBLING THE PIECES

18 Set a stop and cut twelve dowels 81 mm long from 19 mm oak dowel. Sand a 4 mm chamfer on both ends of each dowel.

19 Cut two 50 x 25 mm scraps 660 mm long and two 356 mm long.

Referring to the Support Locations diagram (see page 16), clamp one of each length to the inside face of each chair end. (The strips help centre the ends of the seat and backrest pieces over the 19 mm holes that are drilled later.) To test the locations, position a piece of 50 mm scrap on each support to ensure that the holes in the end pieces will centre on the ends of the seat pieces (B, C) and cleats (E).

20 Referring to the End View diagram (see page 16), position the seat pieces with the help of a second person. Slip the 10 mm spacers between the pieces to ensure that the gap is consistent. Clamp the seat pieces firmly between the chair ends.

21 Chuck a 19 mm spade bit into the drill. Using the previously bored holes in the end sections as guides, bore a pair of 38 mm deep holes squarely into each seat piece end.

22 Immediately after boring the first hole, insert one of the 81 mm long dowels into the hole to help steady the seat piece when you bore the next hole. Make sure that you do not insert the dowel more than 13 mm into the hole drilled into the seat piece, as you may have trouble removing it.

23 Repeat the procedure to position and drill the 81 mm holes in both ends of the backrest cleats (E).

24 Remove one of the 81 mm long dowels. With a small brush, coat the inside of the hole with woodworking adhesive. Using a rubber-tipped mallet to prevent marring the chamfered end, slowly drive the dowel into the hole until just the chamfered end protrudes. Be careful not to drive the dowels too far, as they are difficult to back out.

25 Wipe off any excess glue immediately. Repeat the above procedure for each dowel. After the glue has dried, remove the clamps.

ADDING THE ARMRESTS

26 From 19 mm timber, cut two pieces 610 x 76 mm for the armrests (G).

27 Referring to the Armrest diagram (see page 17), mark the profile on one piece and cut it to shape. Use the first piece as a template to mark the shape on the second armrest and then cut the piece to shape.

28 Mark the hold centrepoints and drill and counterbore the holes. Screw the armrests to the tops of the end assemblies (A).

29 Plane or resaw a piece of timber to 11 mm thick and use a plug cutter to cut 10 mm diameter plugs. Plug the holes and sand the plugs flush with the top of each armrest.

FINISHING

30 Sand the entire chair, forming a slight round-over on all of the edges.

31 If you decide to paint your chair, an oil-based enamel or water-based latex will provide outdoor protection. Apply a prime coat that is compatible with the top coat and make sure that you apply several coats to the porous end grain. To achieve a more natural look, finish the chair with an exterior house stain and then apply several coats of spar varnish.

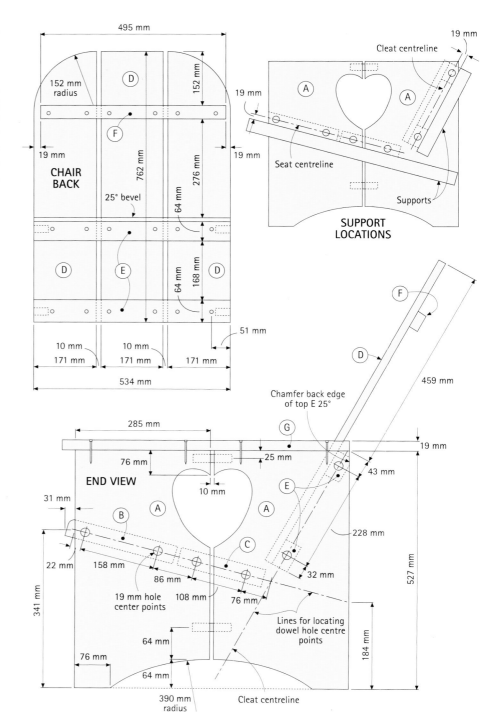

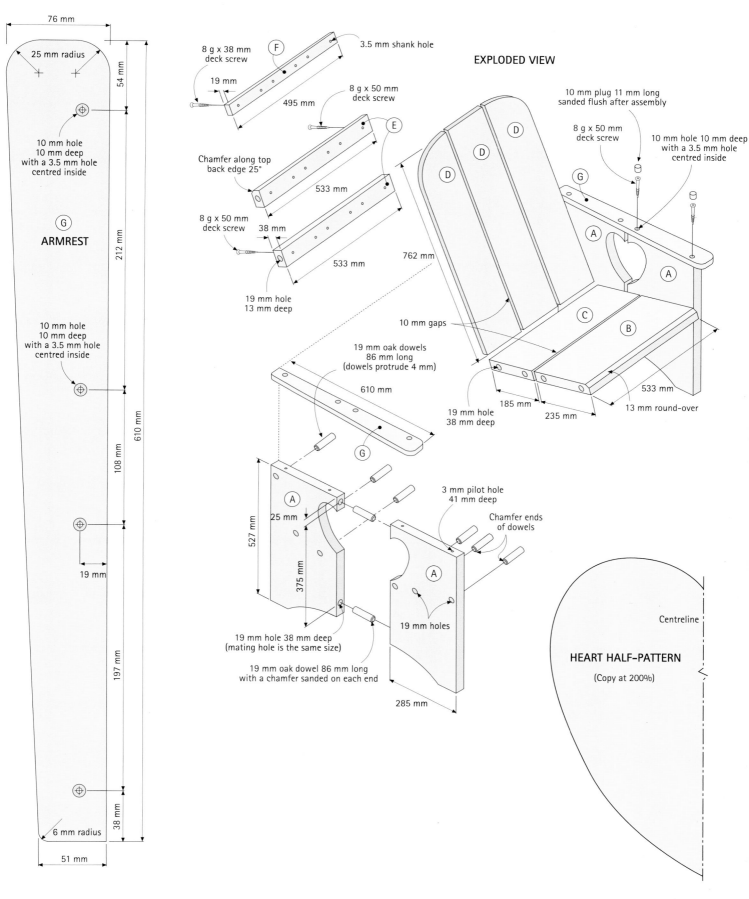

76 mm

25 mm radius

54 mm

10 mm hole
10 mm deep
with a 3.5 mm hole
centred inside

(G)

ARMREST

212 mm

10 mm hole
10 mm deep
with a 3.5 mm hole
centred inside

610 mm

108 mm

19 mm

197 mm

38 mm

6 mm radius

51 mm

8 g x 38 mm
deck screw

(F)

3.5 mm shank hole

19 mm

495 mm

8 g x 50 mm
deck screw

(E)

Chamfer along top
back edge 25°

533 mm

8 g x 50 mm
deck screw

38 mm

533 mm

19 mm hole
13 mm deep

EXPLODED VIEW

10 mm plug 11 mm long
sanded flush after assembly

8 g x 50 mm
deck screw

10 mm hole 10 mm deep
with a 3.5 mm hole
centred inside

(D)

(D)

(D)

(D)

(G)

(A)

(A)

762 mm

10 mm gaps

(C)

(B)

533 mm

185 mm

235 mm

13 mm round-over

19 mm hole
38 mm deep

19 mm oak dowels
86 mm long
(dowels protrude 4 mm)

610 mm

(G)

527 mm

(A)

25 mm

375 mm

3 mm pilot hole
41 mm deep

Chamfer ends
of dowels

(A)

19 mm holes

19 mm hole 38 mm deep
(mating hole is the same size)

19 mm oak dowel 86 mm long
with a chamfer sanded on each end

285 mm

Centreline

HEART HALF–PATTERN

(Copy at 200%)

Comfy Country Bench

This simple but pleasing bench requires only a small investment in materials and a couple of evenings spent in the workshop. Use it indoors for informal seating or place it outdoors to enjoy a view of the garden.

Quick and easy to make, the bench is equally at home indoors and outdoors.

BUILDING THE BENCH ENDS

1   From 285 x 38 mm timber, cut the end pieces (A) to a length of 730 mm.

2   Draw a 25 mm grid measuring 250 x 175 mm on heavy paper or thin cardboard. Lay out the Heart Grid Half-pattern (see page 20) and cut the half-heart template to shape.

3   Position the template and trace the half-heart outline 76 mm from the top of each end piece (see the End View diagram, page 20). Cut the outlines to shape on the band saw or with a jigsaw then drum-sand the pieces to remove the saw marks.

4   To join the end pieces (A), clamp each 285 x 38 mm pair together edge to edge, with the top and bottom edges of the pairs flush. Then, referring to the Exploded View diagram (page 20), mark the three dowel hole locations on one face. Remove the clamps and, using a square, transfer the lines to the inside edge of each end piece.

5   Using a portable electric drill, drill 19 mm holes 38 mm deep, centred from edge to edge, making sure that the drill is square to the surface (see the Exploded View diagram, page 20).

6   From 19 mm dowel timber, set a stop and cut six pieces 86 mm in length. Using a belt sander, sand a chamfer on each end.

7   Cut four 10 mm thick scrap spacers. Glue, dowel and clamp both bench ends together, placing the 10 mm spacers between the end pieces so that the gap is consistent on both ends (see the Support Locations diagram, page 20). Save the spacers for use later.

8   Sand a slight round-over on all edges of each bench end.

TIMBER

PART	FINISHED SIZE IN MM			MATERIAL	QUANTITY
	W	T	L		
A ends	285	38	730	O	4
B seat	184	38	1143	O	2
C back	184	38	1143	O	2

Material key: O = dry (seasoned) oregon*

* Pine or treated pine will also work well. Select pieces 305 x 50 mm for the ends and 203 x 50 mm for the seat and back. If you have trouble locating straight and uncupped timber, edge-join narrower pieces to width.

OTHER MATERIALS

- Two 19 x 900 mm lengths of dowel
- Slow-set epoxy or resorcinol for use of bench outdoors, or woodworking adhesive for indoor use
- Exterior house stain or exterior primer and paint for use of bench outdoors or stain and polyurethane for indoor use

TOOLS

- Table saw
- Band saw
- Drill
- Drill bit: 19 mm
- Drum sander
- Belt sander
- Router
- Router bit: 13 mm round-over
- Orbital sander

Substitute other tools or equipment as desired. Additional common hand tools and clamps may be required.

Always observe the safety precautions in the owner's manual when using a tool or a piece of machinery.

9 From 184 x 38 mm timber, cut the two seat pieces (B) and backrest pieces (C) (see the Timber list, above).

10 Select one seat piece for the front and rout a 13 mm round-over on the top front edge.

MARKING AND DRILLING THE DOWEL HOLES

11 Referring to the End View diagram (see page 20), mark a pair of intersecting lines for locating the dowel-hole centre points on the outside face of each bench end.

12 Locate and mark the eight dowel-hole centre points on the lines on each bench card.

13 Bore 19 mm holes through the bench ends at the marked centre points, backing the timber with scrap to prevent chip-out. (Before drilling the first holes clamp a piece of 100 x 50 mm scrap on the inside face then, repositioning the scrap each time you drill, make the other four holes.)

ASSEMBLING THE PIECES

14 From 19 mm dowel timber, set a stop and cut 16 dowels 80 mm long. Sand a 15 mm chamfer on both ends of each dowel.

15 Cut four 50 x 25 mm scraps to 660 mm long. Referring to the Support Locations diagram (page 20), clamp two strips to the inside face of each bench end. (The strips help centre the seat and backrest pieces over the 19 mm holes that are drilled later.) To test the locations, position a piece of scrap 184 x 38 mm timber on each strip to ensure that the holes will centre in the end of the timber.

16 With the help of a second person position the seat pieces (see the End View diagram, page 20). Slip the 10 mm spacers between the pieces to form a consistent gap. Then, referring to the step 16 illustration (right), clamp the seat pieces firmly between the bench ends. Chuck a 19 mm bit into the drill. Using the previously drilled holes in the end sections as guides, drill a pair of 38 mm deep holes squarely into each seat piece.

17 As soon as you have drilled the first hole, insert one of the 80 mm long dowels just 13 mm into the hole to help steady the seat piece.

18 Repeat the procedure above to drill the 19 mm holes in both ends of the backrest pieces.

19 Remove one of the 80 mm long dowels. With a small brush, coat the inside of the hole with glue. Using a rubber-tipped mallet to prevent marring the chamfered dowel end, slowly drive the dowel into the hole until just the

chamfered end protrudes. Be careful not to drive the dowels too far, as they will be difficult to back out. Wipe off any excess glue immediately with a damp cloth. Repeat the procedure for each remaining dowel. After the glue has dried completely, remove the clamps.

FINISHING

20 Sand the entire bench, forming a slight round-over on all edges.

21 If the bench is to have an outdoor setting and you want to reveal the grain of the wood, finish it with an exterior house stain. If you intend to paint the bench, apply an exterior primer followed by two coats of exterior paint. If the bench is to be used indoors, apply regular stain and a clear finish such as polyurethane, or use an interior primer and paint.

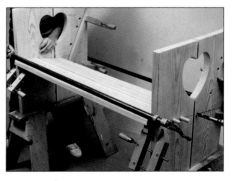

STEP 16 Position the two seat and two back pieces on the support strips and clamp them in place between the end pieces. Then, using the previously drilled holes in the bench ends as guides, drill dowel holes 38 mm deep into the seat pieces.

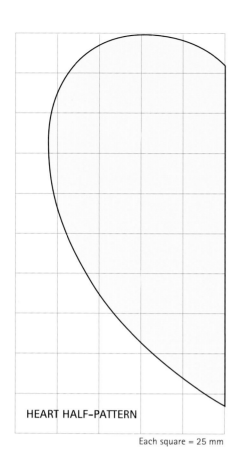

HEART HALF-PATTERN

Each square = 25 mm

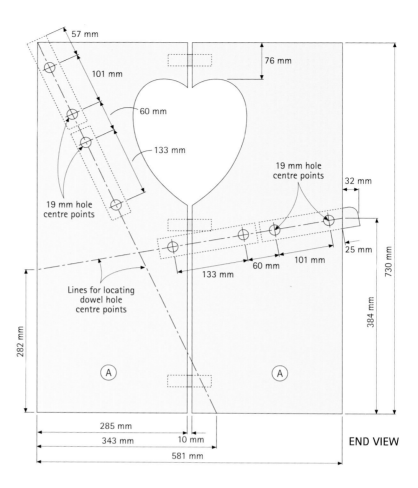

57 mm

101 mm

60 mm

133 mm

19 mm hole
centre points

19 mm hole
centre points

32 mm

76 mm

730 mm

25 mm

384 mm

282 mm

Lines for locating
dowel hole
centre points

133 mm

60 mm

101 mm

(A)   (A)

285 mm

343 mm

10 mm

581 mm

END VIEW

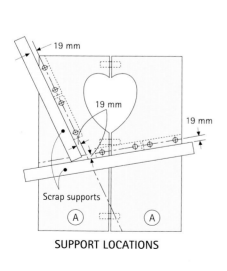

19 mm

19 mm

19 mm

Scrap supports

(A)   (A)

SUPPORT LOCATIONS

EXPLODED VIEW

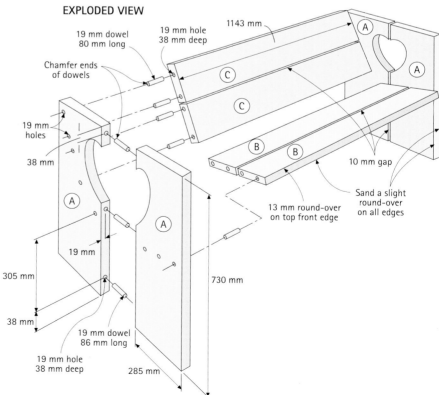

19 mm dowel
80 mm long

19 mm hole
38 mm deep

1143 mm

Chamfer ends
of dowels

(A)

(A)

19 mm
holes

38 mm

(C)

(C)

(B)

(B)

10 mm gap

Sand a slight
round-over
on all edges

13 mm round-over
on top front edge

305 mm

(A)

19 mm

730 mm

38 mm

19 mm dowel
86 mm long

19 mm hole
38 mm deep

285 mm

Candle Stand

Once used solely as a platform for light, these days a candle stand chiefly has a decorative function or is used to support a floral arrangement. A baluster forms the turned pedestal in this stand, to save you the trouble of turning the pedestal yourself.

The stand's painted antique finish gives it an authentic, old-world look.

TIMBER

PART	FINISHED SIZE IN MM			MATERIAL	QUANTITY
	W	T	L		
A leg	70	20	310	P	4
B spindle	40	40	710	P	1
C* top	228	20	254	E-JP	1
D cleats	20	20	80	P	2
E cleats	20	20	40	P	2

Material key: P = pine, E-JP = edge-joined pine

* Edge-join two 127 x 20 mm pieces of pine, 254 mm long to form a circular piece with a 228 mm diameter.

OTHER MATERIALS

- Eight 10 x 38 mm pieces of dowel
- Panel pins: 30 mm, 40 mm
- Woodworking adhesive

TOOLS

- Table saw
- Band saw
- Sanders: belt, disc
- Drill
- Drill bit: 10 mm
- Router
- Router bits: 3 mm round-over, 13 mm round-over
- Dowel jig
- Orbital sander

Substitute other tools or equipment as desired. Additional common hand tools and clamps may be required.

Always observe the safety precautions in the owner's manual when using a tool or a piece of equipment.

CONSTRUCTING THE LEGS

The candle stand is designed to support candles and small objects. If you want to use the stand for larger items, increase the spread of the legs and the diameter of the top to give it greater stability.

1 Using tracing paper or a photocopier, make a copy of the Full-size Leg Pattern (see page 22). Cut the paper pattern to shape and use it as a template to mark four leg outlines on 20 mm pine. (To make the template easier to trace around, glue the paper copy to 3 mm hardboard with spray-on adhesive and band saw a hardboard template to shape.)

2 Band saw the legs (A) to shape. Using double-sided tape, tape together the legs, face-to-face, with the edges and ends flush. Referring to the Step 2 illustration (below), use the round end of a stationary or belt sander to sand the edges of the legs flush.

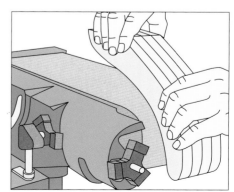

STEP 2 Sand the edges of the legs flush with the round end of the sander.

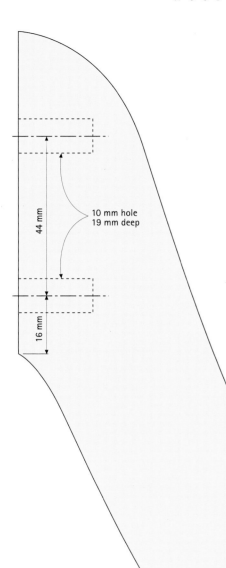

10 mm hole
19 mm deep

44 mm

16 mm

Ⓐ

FULL-SIZE LEG PATTERN

3 Using a square, mark the dowel-hole locations on each leg. Separate the legs and remove the double-sided tape.

4 Referring to the Step 4 illustration (right), with a dowelling jig, drill 10 mm holes 19 mm deep where marked on the Full-size Leg Pattern (see page 22).

5 Referring to the Exploded View Diagram (see page 23), rout or sand a 3 mm round-over on all edges of each leg, except those edges that will fit against the baluster. Then sand each of the legs smooth.

ASSEMBLING THE PEDESTAL

6 You could turn the pedestal yourself but if you can't turn buy a 762 x 50 x 50 mm baluster. Crosscut the top end for a 41 mm finished length.

7 Referring to the Exploded View diagram (see page 23), mark reference centrelines on the bottom of the pedestal. Mark a second line perpendicular to the first line and 19 mm from the bottom of the pedestal.

8 Insert a pair of 10 mm dowel centres into the dowel holes in one leg. Align the dowel centres on the reference lines and squeeze the pieces together to transfer the hole centre points to the pedestal. Drill 10 mm holes 22 mm deep into the pedestal where marked. Sand the pedestal smooth.

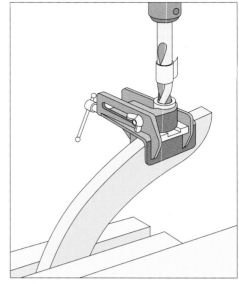

STEP 4 Use a dowelling jig to drill 10 mm holes 19 mm deep.

ADDING THE LEGS

9 Glue a pair of 10 x 38 mm dowel pins in each leg. Referring to the Step 9 illustration (see page 23), clamp a handscrew clamp to each leg. (To prevent the clamp from slipping, wrap sandpaper between the leg and clamp.)

10 Using a pair of quick action clamps, clamp two legs to the pedestal by placing the clamp jaws on the handscrew clamps. To help keep the legs parallel, clamp a piece of scrap timber to the legs.

11 After the glue dries, remove the clamps and redrill the remaining four holes in the baluster to 22 mm deep. (The dowel pins installed with the first two legs reduce the depth of the holes.)

12 Using the procedure described above, glue, dowel and clamp the remaining two legs to the pedestal.

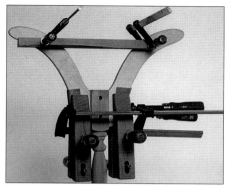

STEP 9   Use handscrew clamps to provide the flat surfaces necessary to align the legs with quick action clamps.

MAKING THE TOP

13 Edge-join two 127 x 20 mm pieces of flat timber to 254 mm long. (Avoid using one solid piece of timber for the top, as it will cup over time.)

14 Draw diagonals to find the centre then use a compass to mark a 228 mm circle (114 mm radius) on the top. Band saw the top to shape, cutting just outside the marked line. To form the finished shape, sand to the line with a disc sander.

15 Rout a bead on the top edge of the round top. Then finish-sand the pedestal assembly and top smooth.

16 Cut four mounting cleats (D, E) (see the Exploded View diagram, right). Glue and nail the cleats to the pedestal with panel pins. Then glue and nail the pedestal and cleats, centred on the bottom side of the top.

FINISHING

17 Apply a paint finish of your choice to the candle stand. To reproduce the painted antique finish on the stand, refer to the techniques described in the candle box project (see page 107). A walnut stain, clear lacquer, cajun red paint, soldier blue paint, mahogany gel stain and satin polyurethane were applied to the stand for this project. The top of the candlestand was given a natural, aged wood finish. To acheive this look, the top must first be distressed and then a number of finishes applied. Follow steps 26 to 32 in the punched-tin pie safe project (see page 75).

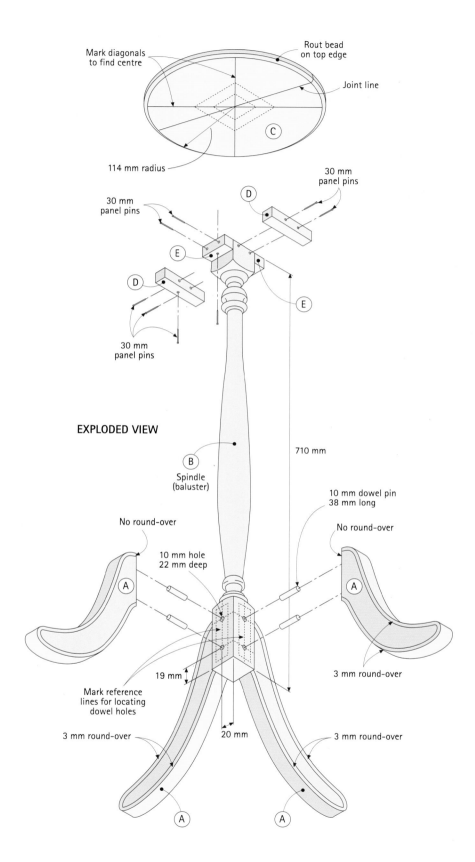

Shaker Simplicity Chairs

The ladder-back chair is the best known of all the superb Shaker designs. This version derives from a Harvard Shaker chair built around 1850. The seat has been raised a little for comfort and the finials removed from the back for simplicity.

CONSTRUCTING A CHAIR–LEG JIG AND DRILL GUIDE

1 Before you begin to build the chair, make a chair-leg jig and drill guide to help you to drill and rout the holes and mortises in the chair legs accurately. From 19 mm plywood, cut the chair-leg jig parts (A, B, C, D) (see the Timber list, page 25). (To form the 13 mm thick layer, you could resaw a piece of 19 mm thick plywood or use 13 mm plywood.)

2 Referring to the Chair-leg Jig End View diagram (see page 26), glue and nail the bottom three layers together (A, B, C), with the inside edges and ends flush. So that the 32 mm-diameter leg dowels fit snugly, make sure the gap between parts B and C are exactly 32 mm for the entire length of the jig.

3 For the jig to work correctly, you must position the top two layers of the jig (D) so that the router will be centred over the 32 mm recess (and so over the chair-leg dowels). (Refer to the Chair-leg Jig End View diagram, page 26.) Glue and nail the top layers into position.

4 Referring to the Chair-leg Jig diagram (page 26), lay out and number the reference lines on the jig.

5 From 19 mm solid maple, cut the dowel clamp (E) (see the Timber list, page 25). Then by using carbon paper, transfer the centrelines for the 32 mm hole, the two 3.5 mm holes and the reference marks A, B and C from the Dowel Clamp diagram (see page 26) to the solid timber.

6 Drill the 32 mm hole and cut a 3 mm wide slot to the 32 mm hole. Drill and countersink the two 3.5 mm holes.

7 Centre the hole in the dowel clamp against the 32 mm wide recess and screw the clamp to the end of the chair-leg

With its comfortable, woven seat and natural finish, the chair is the perfect companion for a kitchen table.

TIMBER

PART	FINISHED SIZE IN MM			MATERIAL	QUANTITY
	W	T	L		
JIG AND DRILL GUIDE					
A bottom layer	227	19	1170	P	1
B second layer	95	19	1170	P	2
C third layer	95	13	1170	P	2
D top layers	38	19	1170	P	4
E dowel clamp	38	19	57	M	1
F drill guide	*	19	279	P	2
SHAKER CHAIR					
A rear legs		32 (diameter)	984	OD	2
B front legs		32 (diameter)	336	OD	2
C top slat	89	27	330	O	1
D middle slat	83	27	330	O	1
E bottom slat	70	27	330	O	1
F rear rail		25 (diameter)	336	OD	1
G rear rungs		19 (diameter)	336	OD	2
H front rail		25 (diameter)	425	OD	1
I front rungs		19 (diameter)	425	OD	2
J side rails		25 (diameter)	330	OD	2
K side rungs		19 (diameter)	330	OD	4

The width marked with an * will depend on the diameter of the router base. Refer to the Drill Guide diagrams (page 27) for information on determining this width.

Material key: P = plywood, M = maple, OD = oak dowel, O = oak

Note: The specifications above are for building a single chair. If you intend to make additional chairs, machine all identical pieces at the same time to ensure uniformity.

OTHER MATERIALS

- Carbon paper
- 30 mm panel pins
- 8 g x 38 mm flathead wood screws
- Woodworking adhesive
- 22 m pure cotton webbing
- Foam cushion
- Tacks
- Finish

TOOLS

- Table saw
- Band saw
- Drill
- Drill press
- Drill bits: 2.5 mm, 3.5 mm, 6 mm
- Forstner bits: 16 mm, 19 mm, 32 mm
- Router
- Router bits: 13 mm straight bit, V-groove bit
- Belt sander
- Disc sander
- Orbital sander
- Rubber mallet
- Hammer

Substitute other tools or equipment as desired. Additional common hand tools and clamps may be required.

Always observe the safety precautions in the owner's manual when using a tool or a piece of machinery.

nearest the G hole and drill the angled holes A and D.

CONSTRUCTING THE CHAIR

13 Select the two straightest long dowels for the back legs (A) (nearly all of them will have a slight bow). To make sure both back legs bend towards the back, lay the dowels on a flat surface and place the bows so that they curve outwards (see the Positioning the Bows diagram, page 29). Mark a reference line on one end of each dowel at the 6 o'clock position and write RR (the initials for right rear) on the same end as the reference line on one dowel and LR (for left rear) on the second dowel.

14 Slide the right rear dowel into the 32 mm recess in the chair-leg jig and into the dowel clamp until the marked end of the right rear dowel is flush with the outside face of the dowel clamp. Rotate the dowel to align the reference line on the dowel with reference line A on the dowel clamp. The top edge of the dowel should be flush with the top face of part C of the chair-leg jig. (You may need to tap the dowel in place with a rubber mallet.)

15 With the assistance of a handscrew clamp, tighten the dowel clamp to prevent the dowel from turning the chair-leg jig when drilling the other holes.

jig (see the Chair-leg Jig End View diagram, page 26).

8 Make the drill guide from 19 mm plywood. Cut the two guide pieces (F) as wide as the diameter of your router base and 279 mm long.

9 Glue and nail the pieces together with the edges and ends flush. When the adhesive has dried, scrape off the excess and check the fit of the guide in the chair-leg jig.

10 Referring to the Drill Guide Top View (page 27), mark a centreline along the length of the drill guide. Draw reference lines perpendicular to the

centreline to locate centre points for the 6 mm, 16 mm and 19 mm holes and mark the letters and hole sizes on each of the reference lines.

11 Using dowel drill bits and the drill press, bore the non-angled holes (B, E, G) through the guide.

12 Referring to the Boring the Angled Holes diagram (see page 27), cut a pair of wedge-shaped blocks to help you bore the angled holes. Position the blocks under the drill guide on your drill-press table. With the wide ends of the blocks nearest the end of the drill guide with hole A, drill the angled holes C and F. Rotate the blocks so the widest ends are

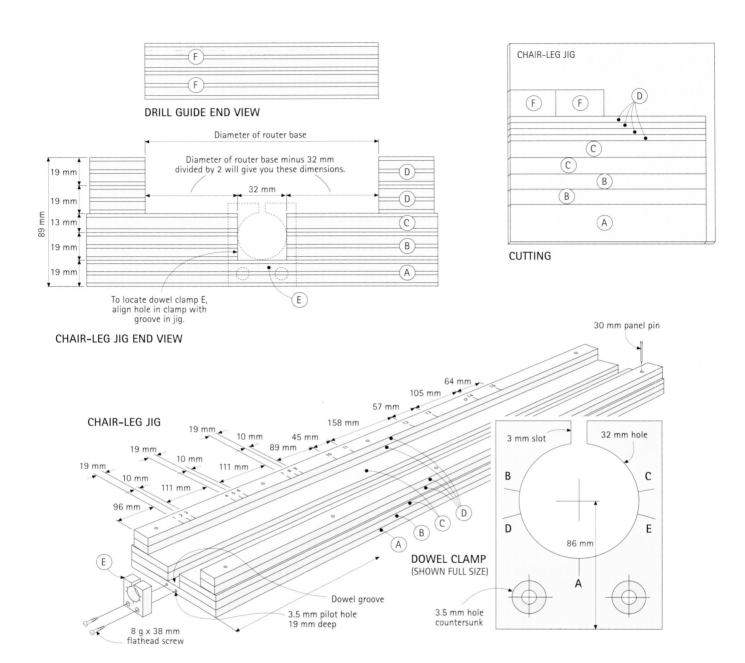

DRILL GUIDE END VIEW

CHAIR-LEG JIG

CUTTING

Diameter of router base

Diameter of router base minus 32 mm divided by 2 will give you these dimensions.

32 mm

89 mm

19 mm
19 mm
13 mm
19 mm
19 mm

To locate dowel clamp E, align hole in clamp with groove in jig.

CHAIR-LEG JIG END VIEW

CHAIR-LEG JIG

19 mm
10 mm
111 mm
96 mm

19 mm
10 mm
111 mm

19 mm
10 mm
89 mm
45 mm

158 mm
57 mm
105 mm
64 mm

30 mm panel pin

E

8 g x 38 mm flathead screw

Dowel groove

3.5 mm pilot hole 19 mm deep

DOWEL CLAMP (SHOWN FULL SIZE)

3 mm slot

32 mm hole

86 mm

A

3.5 mm hole countersunk

STEP 16 *Align the 16 mm hole (reference line B) in the drill guide with the marked number 1 on the chair-leg jig and drill a 16 mm deep hole.*

16 Referring to the Step 16 illustration (left), position the drill guide in the chair-leg jig, aligning reference line B on the drilling guide with the marked number 1 on the chair-leg jig. Clamp the guide to the chair-leg jig. Using a 16 mm dowel bit, bore 16 mm deep into the dowel. To prevent enlarging or changing the angle of the holes in the drill guide, lower the bit through the hole until it makes contact with the dowel. Start the drill and bore the hole. Stop the drill before removing it from the drill guide. To drill to the correct depth, wrap tape around the bit.

STEP 18 *Lower the 8 mm straight bit into the 6 mm hole and rout between a pair of holes to form the 8 mm wide mortises for the backrest slats.*

17 Referring to the Drilling Guide chart (see page 28), move the drill guide to the second setting (B4), and drill a second 16 mm hole. Continue moving the guide along the jig to drill holes E7, G10, G11, G12, G13, G14 and G15 to the sizes listed in the Drilling Guide chart.

18 To create the 13 mm deep mortises for the chair-back slats, chuck an 8 mm straight bit into your router. Referring to the Step 18 illustration (see page 26), slowly lower the rotating bit into one 6 mm hole and rout to the next 6 mm hole. Be sure to grasp the router firmly to prevent it from jerking when entering the second 6 mm hole. Repeating this procedure, form the other mortises.

19 Remove the handscrew clamp from the dowel clamp. Twist the chair-leg dowel until the marked reference line on the end of the dowel aligns with reference line C on the dowel clamp. Again, secure the dowel in the dowel clamp. Referring to the Drilling Guide chart, drill holes C2, C5 and F8 for the right rear dowel.

20 Remove the right rear leg from the jig and cut the top end so that the leg's finished length is 984 mm. Referring to the Drilling Guide chart, follow the same procedure used above to drill the holes in the left rear leg.

21 Cut the front legs (B) to lengths of 445 mm. Mark a reference line on one end of each leg and, referring to the Drilling Guide chart, bore the holes in both of the legs.

SHAPING THE SLATS

22 From 27 mm oak, cut the top slat (C), middle slat (D) and bottom slat (E) (see the Timber list, page 25).

23 Referring to the Backrest Slat Top View diagram (see page 29), cut a 13 mm rebate 19 mm deep across the ends on the back face of each slat blank. Then transfer the cut lines to a piece of 6 mm hardboard, cut the hardboard to shape and use it as a template to mark all the cut lines on the top edge of each slat blank.

24 Band saw the front and back of each slat to shape (see Step 1 of the Shaping the Slats diagram, page 29).

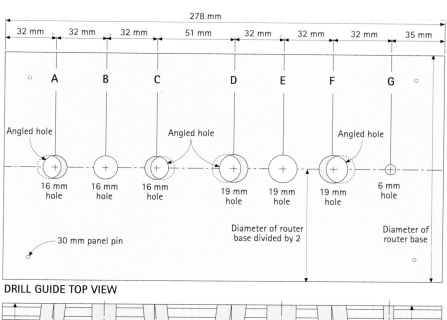

DRILL GUIDE TOP VIEW

DRILL GUIDE SECTION VIEW

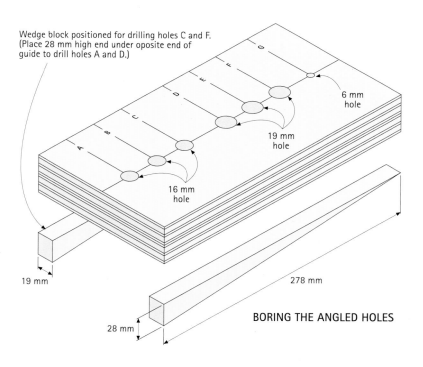

Wedge block positioned for drilling holes C and F. (Place 28 mm high end under opposite end of guide to drill holes A and D.)

BORING THE ANGLED HOLES

DRILLING GUIDE

DOWEL-CLAMP SETTING	JIG-GUIDE SETTING	HOLE SIZE IN MM
RIGHT REAR LEG		
A	B1	16
A	B4	16
A	E7	19
A	G10	6
A	G11	6
A	G12	6
A	G13	6
A	G14	6
A	G15	6
C	C2	16
C	C5	16
C	F8	19
LEFT REAR LEG		
A	B1	16
A	B4	16
A	E7	19
A	G10 to G15	6
Same drilling sequence as right rear leg		
B	C2	16
B	C5	16
B	F8	19
RIGHT FRONT LEG		
A	B1	16
A	B4	16
A	E7	19
D	A3	16
D	A6	16
D	D9	19
LEFT FRONT LEG		
A	B1	16
A	B4	16
A	E7	19
E	A3	16
E	A6	16
E	D9	19

Tape the front and back scrap pieces onto the band-sawed slat. This will make

25 Referring to the Backrest Slat Front View diagram (page 29), mark the cut line on the scrap front face of each slat. Referring to Step 2 of the Shaping the Slats diagram (page 29), use a piece of 6 mm hardboard as a template to mark the curved portion along the top of each slat and band saw the top edge of each slat to shape. Remove the pieces of scrap.

26 Referring to the Step 26 illustration (left), sand each slat to remove the saw marks.

marking and cutting the top edge of the slats easier.

STEP 26   Sand the front and back surfaces of the backrest slats on a stationary or belt sander to remove the saw marks.

27 Sand a slight round-over along the top and bottom of the tenons on each slat (see the Chair diagram, page 31). Check that the slats fit the mortises in the rear chair legs.

ROUTING THE TENONS IN THE RAILS AND RUNGS

28 From 19 mm and 25 mm dowels, cut the rear rail (F) and rungs (G), the front members (H, I) and the side members (J, K) to size (see the Timber list, page 25).

29 Cut and shape a V-grooved block (see the V-Groove Block diagram, page 31).

30 Referring to Step 1 on the Routing the Tenons diagram (page 31), chuck a 13 mm straight bit into a table-mounted router and rotate the dowel by hand to rout 3 mm into the ends of rails F, H, J. Check the fit of the tenons in their mating holes. (You could practise routing scrap dowel timber until you have the settings right.)

31 Adjust the router bit to make a 1.5 mm cut, leaving a 16 mm tenon on the ends of each 19 mm dowel (see Step 2 on the Routing the Tenons diagram, page 31). Follow the procedure used for the rails to rout the tenons on the chair rungs (G, I, K).

32 Switch to a V-groove bit and adjust the height to rout the chamfers on the 25 mm dowels (see Step 3 on the Routing the Tenons diagram, page 31). Then, adjust the bit height for the 19 mm dowels and rout their chamfers.

SHAPING THE CHAIR LEG ENDS

33 Cut the sanding guide from 38 mm thick timber (see the Making and Using the Sanding Guide diagram, page 30).

34 Clamp the guide to your disc-sander table (you could use a belt sander on a stand instead of the disc-sander) and sand a 10 degree chamfer on the top end of each chair leg (A, B). Then sand a 38 mm taper on the bottom of each chair leg.

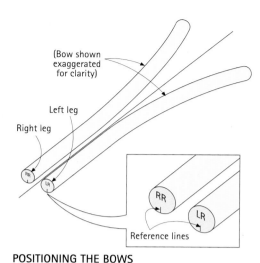

(Bow shown
exaggerated
for clarity)

Left leg

Right leg

RR

LR

RR

LR

Reference lines

POSITIONING THE BOWS

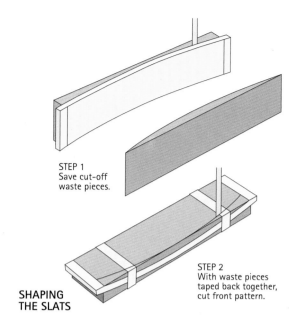

STEP 1
Save cut-off
waste pieces.

STEP 2
With waste pieces
taped back together,
cut front pattern.

**SHAPING
THE SLATS**

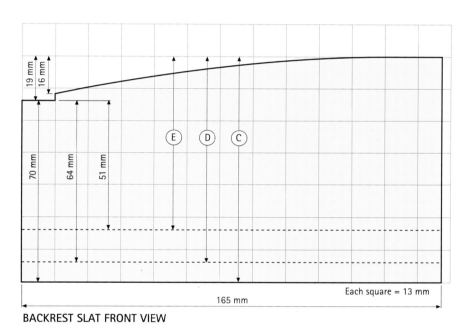

19 mm

16 mm

70 mm

64 mm

51 mm

E   D   C

165 mm

Each square = 13 mm

BACKREST SLAT FRONT VIEW

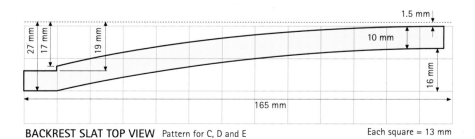

1.5 mm

27 mm

17 mm

19 mm

10 mm

16 mm

165 mm

BACKREST SLAT TOP VIEW Pattern for C, D and E

Each square = 13 mm

MAKING AND USING THE SANDING GUIDE

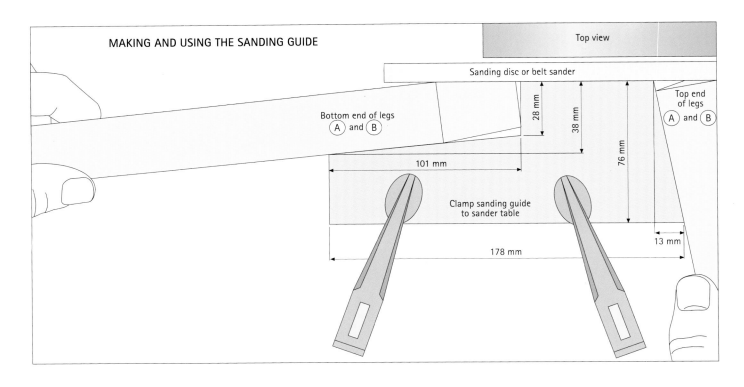

Top view

Sanding disc or belt sander

Bottom end of legs Ⓐ and Ⓑ

Top end of legs Ⓐ and Ⓑ

28 mm

38 mm

76 mm

101 mm

Clamp sanding guide to sander table

13 mm

178 mm

WEAVING THE SEAT

STEP 1
Cut a 50 mm radius from the front corners of the foam cushion. Tape the cushion in place.

STEP 2
Nail the end of the fabric tape to the bottom side of the top back rail. Wet the cut end of the tape with glue to prevent fraying.

STEP 3
Pull the warp over the top of the front top rail, then back around under the bottom of the rear rail. Repeat all the way across the width of the chair, keeping the warps tight.

STEP 4
Nail the end of the twelth warp to the bottom of the rail. Remove the cushion tape.

STEP 5
Nail the end of the weft to the bottom side of the side rail.

STEP 6
Weave the weft through the warps, keeping the weft tight.

STEP 7
Nail the end of the eleventh weft to the bottom side of the side rail.

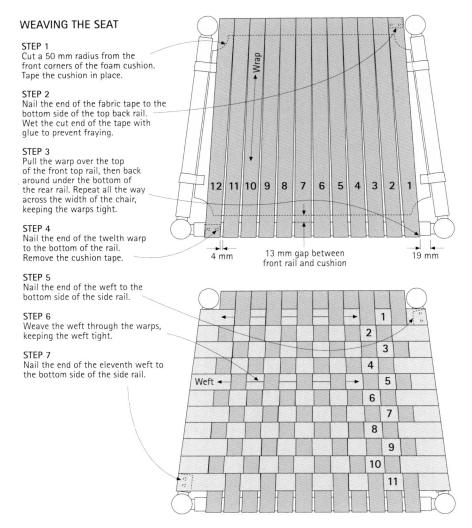

Wrap

12 11 10 9 8 7 6 5 4 3 2 1

4 mm

13 mm gap between front rail and cushion

19 mm

Weft

1 2 3 4 5 6 7 8 9 10 11

ASSEMBLING AND FINISHING THE CHAIR

35 On a flat surface, glue and clamp together the chair-back assembly (A, C, D, E, F, G). (To prevent denting the dowels, use clamp blocks.)

36 With a framing square, check for square and wipe off excess glue with a damp rag. Then, using the same procedure, assemble the front (B, H, I).

37 Using band clamps, glue the side rails and rungs (J, K) between the front and back assemblies.

38 When the adhesive has dried, remove the clamps and finish-sand the chair. Apply a coat of stain. Follow this with two to three coats of polyurethane.

39 The seat is formed by cutting the corners from a foam cushion and taping the cushion in place on the seat. Cotton tape in nailed to the top back rail and pulled over the top of the front top rail and around the bottom of the rear rail. The seat is woven by nailing tape to the bottom of the side rail and weaving it through the tape pulled over the top of the front rail. For detailed instructions, follow the sequence of steps beside the Weaving the Seat diagram (left).

ROUTING THE TENONS

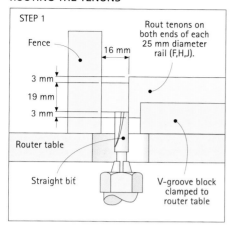

STEP 1

Fence

16 mm

Rout tenons on both ends of each 25 mm diameter rail (F,H,J).

3 mm
19 mm
3 mm

Router table

Straight bit

V-groove block clamped to router table

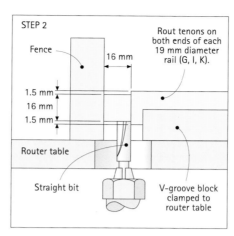

STEP 2

Fence

16 mm

Rout tenons on both ends of each 19 mm diameter rail (G, I, K).

1.5 mm
16 mm
1.5 mm

Router table

Straight bit

V-groove block clamped to router table

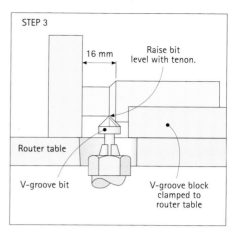

STEP 3

16 mm

Raise bit level with tenon.

Router table

V-groove bit

V-groove block clamped to router table

V-GROOVE BLOCK

19 mm
19 mm

13 mm deep groove (cut with table saw)

90°

19 mm

305 mm

63 mm

CHAIR

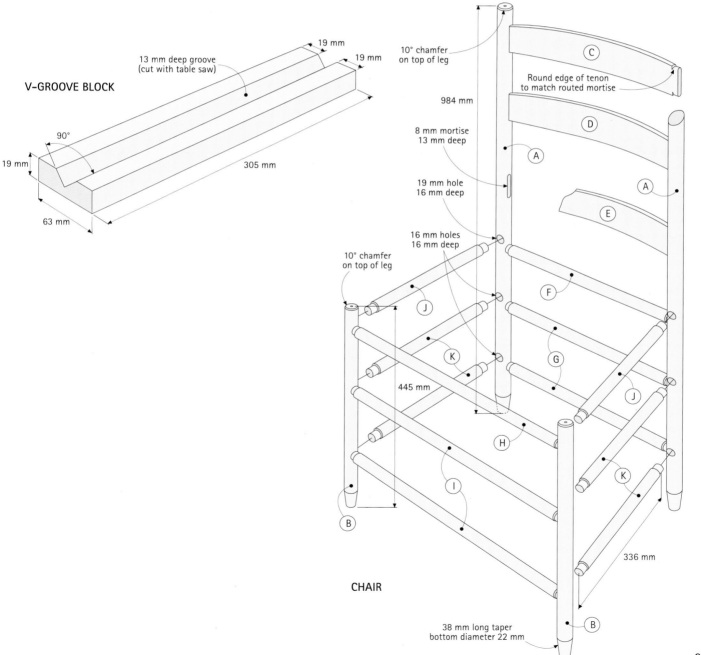

10° chamfer on top of leg

C

Round edge of tenon to match routed mortise

984 mm

D

8 mm mortise 13 mm deep

A

A

19 mm hole 16 mm deep

E

16 mm holes 16 mm deep

F

10° chamfer on top of leg

J

G

J

K

445 mm

H

B

I

336 mm

K

B

38 mm long taper bottom diameter 22 mm

Plate Rack

This practical plate rack has been designed to fit inside an existing cabinet, improving the cabinet's design without compromising its style.

FORMING THE TOP, BOTTOM, END AND SHELF PIECES

1 From 16 mm thick plywood or MDF, cut the top (A) and bottom (B) pieces (see the Timber list, page 33).

2 Fit a router with a 10 mm bit and rout a 6 mm rebate 10 mm deep along one long edge of both the top and bottom pieces for the plywood backing.

3 Cut the two end pieces (C) to size (see the Timber list, page 33). With the router still set, run a stopped rebate along the back edge of both ends, leaving 6 mm on each end. Square out the ends of the rebate with a chisel.

4 Cut a piece of 16 mm thick MDF or plywood to 244 x 950 mm long for the shelf (D). Using an iron, apply a length of edging veneer to the front edge of the shelf and the bottom edges of the ends. Then sand the edges of the veneer smooth and flush with the face of each piece.

5 Draw a line 25 mm in from the front edge and a second line 75 mm in from the back rebated edge of the bottom piece. Then mark the holes for the dowel dividers at 50 mm intervals along each line. With a 13 mm dowel bit, drill each hole 10 mm deep. Wrap masking tape around the bit as a depth guide.

6 Mark and drill the dowel holes in the underside of the shelf piece in the same manner, but place the second row of holes 69 mm in from the back edge.

ASSEMBLING THE RACK

7 To join the unit, mark out dowel holes in the end of the top, bottom and shelf pieces, 50 mm in from each edge and in the centre (8 mm down from the

The size of the plate rack can be adjusted to suit any kitchen cupboard. The plate compartments are formed of lengths of dowel.

TIMBER

PART	FINISHED SIZE IN MM			MATERIAL	QUANTITY
	W	T	L		
A top	250	16	950	Ply or MDF	1
B bottom	250	16	950	Ply or MDF	1
C ends	250	16	565	Ply or MDF	2
D shelf	244	16	950	Ply or MDF	1
E fixing rail	32	19	950	P	1
F back	553	6	970	Ply	1
G trim	25	13	3500*	P	1

* To be cut to length to suit cabinet.

Material key: Ply = plywood, MDF = medium density fibreboard, P = pine

OTHER MATERIALS

- 8 x 30 mm length of pine, beech etc dowel
- Thirty-six 13 x 398 mm lengths of pine dowel
- 2 m iron-on edging tape
- 20 mm panel pins
- Screws: 6 g x 28 mm, 6 g x 40 mm, 6 g x 45 mm
- Paint or lacquer

TOOLS

- Hand saw or mitre drop saw
- Portable electric drill
- Drill bits: 2 mm, 3.5 mm, countersink, 8 mm dowel, 13 mm dowel
- Router
- Router bit: 10 mm rebate
- Four 1200 mm sash or bar clamps

Substitute other tools or equipment as desired. Additional common hand tools and clamps may be required.

Always observe the safety precautions in the owner's manual when using a tool or a piece of machinery.

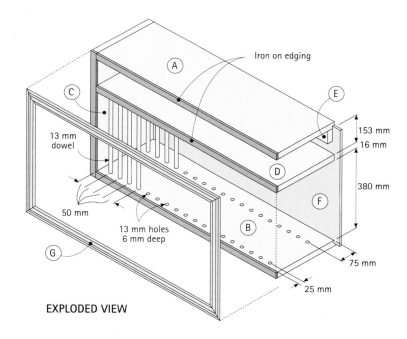

EXPLODED VIEW

Iron on edging

13 mm dowel

50 mm

13 mm holes 6 mm deep

153 mm
16 mm
380 mm
75 mm
25 mm

face). Install an 8 mm dowel bit in the electric drill and drill holes for each of the dowels 20 mm deep.

8 Mark out and drill the matching holes on the inside of the ends. Make sure that the top and bottom pieces are flush on all sides and ensure that the shelf is flush on the front edge and on the sides of the rebates 396 mm from the bottom.

9 Cut the thirty-six dowel dividers to 398 mm long. Chamfer the dowel ends, using sandpaper, so that they fit into their holes easily. Then place a little adhesive in the first of the holes in the base and push a dowel into the hole, tapping it down with a mallet. Fill the remaining holes in the base with dowels in the same manner, then apply adhesive to the holes in the shelf and push onto the upright dowels. Tap down on the shelf with the

mallet to fix the dowels in place, if necessary.

10 Glue the dowels into the ends of the shelf, top and bottom. Place adhesive in the corresponding holes on the ends, then use sash clamps to pull the joints together. Check for square and twist. Wipe off any excess glue with a damp rag.

11 From 19 mm pine, cut a piece 32 x 950 mm long for the fixing rail (E). Run a bead of glue along the edge of the fixing rail and push it under the top, in line with the rebate. Using small clamps to hold the rail in place, drill four 3.5 mm clearance holes through the top. Countersink the holes, then drill a 2 mm pilot hole into the rail and insert 6 g x 40 mm screws. Remove the clamps and wipe off excess glue.

12 Cut the 6 mm thick ply back (F) to size so that it fits neatly into the rebate. Glue and nail it in place with 20 mm panel pins.

13 Referring to the Exploded View diagram (left), cut the trim mould (G) to fit around the face of the rack, mitring it at the corners. Glue and fix it in position, using 20 mm panel pins. Sand all surfaces smooth and apply a finish of your choice.

SECURING THE RACK

14 Hold the rack in position in an existing kitchen cabinet with small clamps. Then, using 6 g x 45 mm screws, screw through the fixing rail into wall studs. Screw through the inside of the cabinet, using 6 g x 28 mm screws.

Window Figures on Stands

Decorate a window at Christmas time with these striking wooden figures. They can be made very economically from scrap MDF and decorated with surplus paint.

CUTTING THE FIGURES

1 Cut three pieces of 16 mm MDF to 150 x 120 mm for the bases (A). With a pencil, starting at a corner, draw a diagonal line across the piece to the opposite corner and repeat this procedure, connecting the other corners, to find the centre (the point where the lines intersect).

2 Scale the Base Pattern (see page 35) to size and transfer it to a piece of heavy cardboard. Cut the outline with scissors and mark the centre.

3 Line the centre of the template up with the centre of the each base piece and trace the outline of the shape onto the face. Cut just outside the shape outline with a jigsaw, then sand the edges smooth back to the line.

4 Using an 8 mm drill bit, drill a hole through the centre of each base. Make sure the the hole is drilled straight so that the stem will stand upright. Sand the face of the base and round over the edges about 3 mm.

5 Observe the following procedure to shape each figure. Cut a piece of 16 mm thick MDF to size (see the Timber list, page 35).

6 Scale the pattern (see page 35) to the correct size, then transfer it to the piece, or, if you intend to make a number of the same figure, onto a piece of cardboard to serve as a template.

7 Using a jigsaw, cut just outside the line of the shape. Take your time

An angel, a hen and a goose make attractive subjects. Paint each one in a single colour to enhance its profile.

TIMBER

PART	FINISHED SIZE IN MM				
	W	T	L	MATERIAL	QUANTITY
A bases	150	16	120	Ply or MDF	3
B goose	240	16	140	Ply or MDF	1
C hen	200	16	140	Ply or MDF	1
D angel	280	16	180	Ply or MDF	1

Material key: Ply = plywood, MDF = medium density fibreboard

OTHER MATERIALS

- Heavy cardboard
- Three 8 x 100 mm dowels
- Woodworking adhesive
- Fine sandpaper
- 20 mm dowel
- Paint or lacquer

TOOLS

- Jigsaw or coping saw
- Scissors
- Sanding cork and sandpaper
- Small file
- Drill
- Drill bits: 8 mm

Substitute other tools or equipment as desired. Additional common hand tools and clamps may be required.

Always observe the safety precautions in the owner's manual when using a tool or a piece of machinery.

with this because the better the edge is sawn, the smaller the amount of sanding required later. Sand the edges of the figure with a piece of fine sandpaper wrapped around a 20 mm dowel.

8 Use a small file to sand the tight places surrounding the corners. Then sand both faces smooth but don't round over the edges (they need to be square and sharp).

9 Referring to the pattern (see right), transfer the position of the stem hole onto the bottom edge of the figure. Drill an 8 mm hole 20 mm deep in the figure's bottom edge. Make sure that the hole is both straight and parallel to the piece's face.

ASSEMBLING AND FINISHING

10 Cut a piece of 8 mm dowel 100 mm long for the stem. Roll each end of the dowel in adhesive, then push one end of the dowel into the hole in the figure and the other end into the hole in the base.

11 Check that the figure is standing upright. Wipe off any excess adhesive with a damp rag. Set the figure aside to let the adhesive dry.

12 Paint the figure a finish and colour of your choice. The figures featured here were given an undercoat, followed by a coat of semi-gloss enamel, a light sanding and a second coat of enamel.

BASE PATTERN

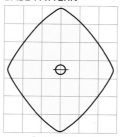

Each square = 20 mm

HEN PATTERN

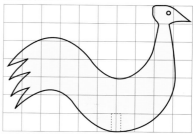

Each square = 20 mm

GOOSE PATTERN

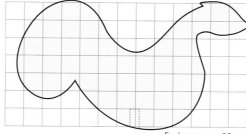

Each square = 20 mm

ANGEL PATTERN

Each square = 20 mm

Coat Cabinet

This handy cabinet provides a spot for hanging coats and bags and somewhere to sit down to remove your shoes. The bench lid flips up for storage.

The cabinet was designed for a room that was 2.85 metres high. To shorten it to fit your room, adjust the space between the bench and the upper cabinet.

CONSTRUCTING THE SIDES

1 From 19 mm pine ply or veneered MDF, cut two pieces 458 x 2100 mm long for the sides (A). Referring to the Side Detail diagram on the Exploded View diagram (page 37), cut a recess in the front edge with your jigsaw. Use a block plane and file to get into the corners and clean up the edges.

2 With the aid of an iron, apply pre-glued edge tape to the front edge. Sand and clean the edge tape flush with the sides.

3 Set a 12 mm rebate cutter into a router and cut a 16 x 10 mm rebate along the inside back edge of each side.

FORMING THE BASE

4 Cut a strip of pine ply or veneered MDF 82 mm wide and cut it into one 952 mm length for the base (B1), and two 439 mm lengths for the base stand (B2).

5 Cut the base (C) to 458 x 952 mm long. Referring to the Exploded View diagram (see page 37), with 38 mm panel pins, glue and nail the base sides to the base. Make sure that all the edges are flush.

ASSEMBLING THE BOX SEAT

6 From 19 mm pine ply or veneered MDF, cut two pieces 305 x 952 mm long for the box sides (D) and two pieces 305 x 400 mm long for the box ends (E). Assemble the box frame by gluing and screwing the sides and ends together, using 6 g x 45 mm screws.

7 Screw the box frame onto the base, keeping the back and ends flush, by applying a bead of glue along the bottom edge of the box frame and inserting three 6 g x 45 mm screws through the base (C) along each edge.

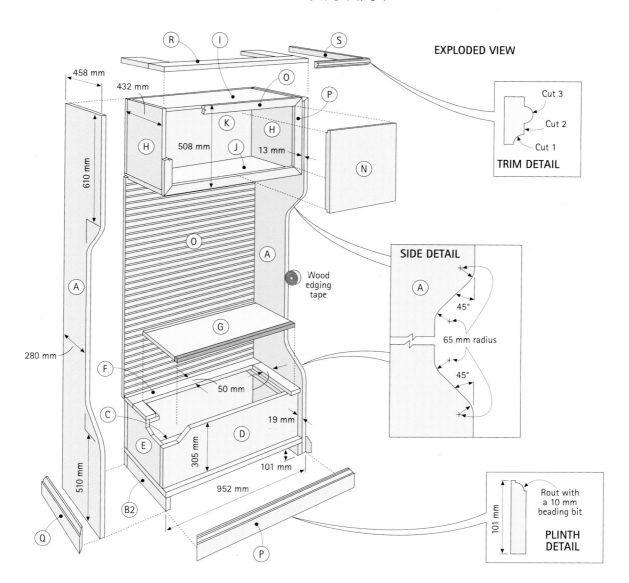

EXPLODED VIEW

TRIM DETAIL

Cut 3
Cut 2
Cut 1

SIDE DETAIL

45°

65 mm radius

45°

Wood edging tape

PLINTH DETAIL

Rout with a 10 mm beading bit

101 mm

458 mm
432 mm
610 mm
508 mm
13 mm
280 mm
510 mm
50 mm
19 mm
305 mm
101 mm
952 mm

8 From the 50 x 3000 mm length of 19 mm pine, cut two pieces 400 mm long for the seat frame (F). Glue and screw the pieces along the top edge, just inside the box, using three screws through each side and one at each end. Ensure that the pieces are flush with the top of the box.

9 From the same length of pine, cut a piece 952 mm long for the back hinge rail. Then cut another two pieces 396 mm long. Run a bead of glue along the top edges of the back and the sides of the box. Using 40 mm panel pins, nail the hinge rail into place so that the ends are flush with the sides of the box but it is 12 mm in from the back of the box. This creates a 12 mm rebate for the lining boards.

10 Nail the 396 mm long pieces securely along the tops of the sides. This should form rebates for the

seat as well as create a 6 mm overhang at the front.

11 Cut the box lid (G) to fit into the rebates and finish flush with the front of the seat frame. Make sure there is approximately 2 mm clearance at each end and 4 mm at the back for the piano hinge. Iron a piece of edging to the front edge.

CONSTRUCTING THE TOP CABINET

12 From 19 mm pine plywood, cut two pieces 432 x 489 mm long for the cabinet sides (H), a piece 432 x 914 mm long for the top (I) and a piece 432 mm x 952 mm long for the bottom (J). Using a router fitted with a 12 mm rebate bit, cut a 6 mm wide rebate 10 mm deep in the back edge of the base, for the lining boards.

13 Assemble the cabinet sides, top and base, inserting three 6 g x 40 mm screws at each joint. Place the sides on top of the base and the top between the sides. Make sure that the front of the cabinet is flush.

14 From 6 mm plywood, cut a piece 498 x 952 mm for the cabinet back (K). Glue and nail it, using 16 mm panel pins, into the rebate at the base of the cabinet.

15 With a mitre drop saw, cut and mitre the cabinet facings (L, M) to fit over the front of the cabinet. Run a bead of glue along the edge of the cabinet and nail the facings into place using 40 mm panel pins.

16 Make the two cabinet doors (N) by cutting two pieces of 19 mm

TIMBER

	FINISHED SIZE IN MM				
PART	W	T	L	MATERIAL	QUANTITY
A sides	458	19	2100	P ply or MDFV	2
B1 base stand	82	19	952	P ply or MDFV	1
B2 base stand	82	19	439	P ply or MDFV	2
C base	458	10	952	P ply or MDFV	1
D box sides	305	19	952	P ply or MDFV	2
E box ends	305	19	400	P ply or MDFV	2
F seat frame	50	19	3000**	P	1
G lid	394	19	848	P ply or MDFV	2
H cabinet sides	432	19	489	P ply or MDFV	2
I cabinet top	432	19	914	P ply or MDFV	1
J cabinet bottom	432	19	952	P ply or MDFV	1
K cabinet back	498	6	952	P ply	1
L cabinet facing	38	13	952	P	2
M cabinet facing	38	13	508	P	2
N door	448	19	445	MDF	2
O back	75	12	972	V-JB	21
P plinth front	101	19	1050	P	1
Q plinth side	101	19	480	P	2
R filler	50	19	2100**	P	1
S trim	32	19	2100*	P	1

* May be replaced with purchased trim of your choice.

** Denotes lineal measurements. Lengths must be cut to suit.

Material key: P ply = pine plywood, MDFV = veneered medium density fibreboard, P = pine, V-JB = V-jointed boards, MDF = medium density fibreboard

OTHER MATERIALS

- 8 m pre-glued iron-on edging
- Piano hinges: One 900 mm, two 450 mm
- Screws: 6 g x 30 mm, 6 g x 45 mm
- Panel pins: 12 mm, 25 mm, 30 mm, 40 mm
- Woodworking adhesive; paint or lacquer

TOOLS

- Jigsaw
- Mitre drop saw
- Drill
- Drill bits: 2 mm, 3.5 mm
- Iron
- Router
- Router bits: 12 mm rebate, 6 mm bead, 16 mm cove

Substitute other tools or equipment as desired. Additional common hand tools and clamps may be required.

Always observe the safety precautions in the owner's manual when using a tool or a piece of machinery.

MDF to 448 x 445 mm long. Then, with a router, cut a 8 mm rebate 13 mm deep in the top and bottom edges. Check that both doors fit and the rebate sits over the cabinet facing. Allow 2 to 3 mm clearance for paint and movement. Plane the edge of the doors to fit, if necessary.

ASSEMBLING THE CABINET

17 Lay one side (A) down onto the workbench with the inside facing up. Place the box into position on the side, keeping the bottom and front edges flush. Then insert two 8 g x 30 mm screws through the inside of the box, just under the seat frame, and into the side. Insert two more 8 g x 30 mm screws through the base stand of the box and into the side.

18 Place the cabinet on its end and into position on the side so that the tops are flush and the rebates line up. Using four 6 g x 30 mm screws, one for each corner, secure the cabinet firmly to the sides.

19 Place the second side onto the assembly and screw it into place in the same way.

20 Measure the distance between the rebates in the back of the cabinet, then cut the beaded lining boards (O) to suit. Glue and nail the boards to the sides with 25 mm panel pins. Wipe excess off excess adhesive with a wet rag.

21 Roll the cabinet over onto its back. Place a 10 mm beading cutter in your router. Rout an ovalo along

one edge of a piece of 19 mm pine 101 x 1050 mm long (see the Plinth Detail diagram on the Exploded View diagram, page 37). Mitre cut it to length so that it will run around the base of the storage box, creating a plinth (P, Q). Glue and nail the plinth pieces into position, with bottom edges flush.

22 From a piece of 19 mm thick pine, 50 mm wide, cut three pieces, one 990 mm long (the width of the cabinet) and two 408 mm long, for the cabinet filler (R). Glue and screw the filler pieces into place around the top of the cabinet, ensuring that they are flush with the outside of the frame.

23 Refer to the Trim Detail diagram on Exploded View diagram (see page 37) to form a piece of 32 x 19 mm thick trim moulding (S), 2100 mm long, if it is unavailable from hardware stores. (Use a piece of 32 x 19 mm thick pine timber and a router with a cover cutter and a bead cutter.)

24 Mitre cut the trim to fit around the top of the cabinet, over the filler piece. Glue and nail it into position, using 30 mm panel pins.

FINISHING

25 Punch all the exposed nail holes and fill with wood stop. Then sand the entire cabinet and apply a finish of your choice.

26 Use lengths of piano hinge to hang the doors and set the lid. You could install the rack described on page 39.

Shaker-style Racks

This handy hat rack, with its Shaker-style wooden pegs, is simple enough to make in a weekend, while the multi-purpose shelf and pegboard can be built any length to meet the requirements of your room. The instructions here are for a shelf that is 850 mm long with four pegs.

Stain the pine to reveal the natural grain or paint it a muted blue to bring a bit of country style to your home.

Building the hat rack

1 Cut a piece of 70 x 16 mm thick pine or MDF 1000 mm long for the back board (A).

2 Sand a small round on all the edges or use a router with a 3 mm round-over bit to shape the edges and remove the sharp corners.

3 Mark the centre of the board, for the centre peg hole. This should be 500 mm in from each end and 35 mm in from the edge.

4 Mark another two holes for the pegs at a distance of 200 mm apart on each side of the centre point.

5 Install a 15 mm Forstner bit in the drill (or a drill bit a size that suits the ends of the shaker pegs). Clamp a scrap of timber securely to the back board. (This is so that the board does not chip.) Then drill the peg holes through the back board.

6 Sand the board smooth using an orbital or a belt sander. Alternatively, wrap a piece of sandpaper around a cork block and use this as a sander.

FINISHING THE RACK

7 Glue the pegs into the holes and wipe off any excess adhesive with a damp rag. Leave the adhesive to dry overnight then paint or lacquer the rack.

MOUNTING THE RACK

8 Mount the rack onto a wall by drilling and screwing through the back board into wall studs or by using an appropriate wall anchor.

TIMBER

PART	FINISHED SIZE IN MM			MATERIAL	QUANTITY
	W	T	L		
A back board	70	16	1000	P or MDF	1
B Shaker-style pegs*		150	200	P	5

* Can be turned on a wood lathe or purchased from woodturning centres and craft shops.

Material key: P = pine

OTHER MATERIALS

- Screws or wall anchors for mounting
- Woodworking adhesive
- Paint or lacquer

TOOLS

- Handsaw or mitre drop saw
- Portable electric drill
- Drill bit: 15 mm Forstner

Substitute other tools or equipment as desired. Additional common hand tools and clamps may be required.

Always observe the safety precautions in the owner's manual when using a tool or a piece of machinery.

Building the shelf and pegboard

1 From 16 mm thick pine or MDF, cut a top piece (A) 100 x 850 mm long (or the required length). Sand a small round on all the edges or use a router with a 3 mm round-over bit to shape the edges and remove the sharp corners.

2 From 19 mm pine or MDF, cut two pieces 90 x 145 mm long, for the shelf supports (B).

3 For each piece, measure 20 mm across the end and down 12 mm towards the opposite end. Referring to the Shelf Support Detail diagram (see page 41), draw a horizontal and a vertical line to bisect this point, then join the two lines together with a third line, in order to give the cutting angle. Cut along the angled line with a jigsaw, then sand or plane the cut edge smooth.

4 Glue and nail the shelf supports and top together using PVA adhesive and 1.6 x 38 mm nails. Place the supports 20 mm in from each shelf end. Make sure they are square to the back edge of the top.

5 Measure the distance between the shelf supports, then cut the back (C) to length from 145 x 19 mm thick pine.

6 If you plan to shape the back, transfer the Back Half-pattern (see page 41) to a piece of stiff cardboard, scaling the pattern to suit the length of the shelf. Cut the pattern out.

7 Square a line across the face of the back at the centre. Line up the end of the pattern with this mark and trace the outline. Flip the pattern over and lay out the

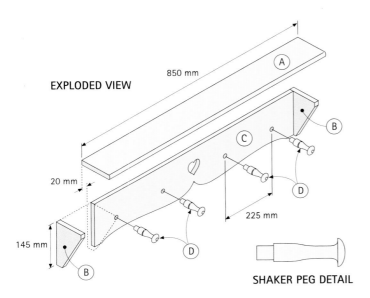

EXPLODED VIEW

850 mm

20 mm

145 mm

225 mm

SHAKER PEG DETAIL

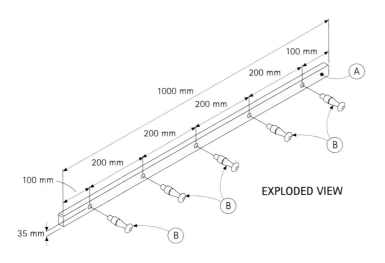

100 mm

200 mm

1000 mm

200 mm

200 mm

200 mm

100 mm

35 mm

EXPLODED VIEW

TIMBER

PART	FINISHED SIZE IN MM			MATERIAL	QUANTITY
	W	T	L		
A top	100	16	850	P or MDF	1
B support	90	19	145	P or MDF	2
C back	145	19	772	P or MDF	1
D Shaker-style pegs*	30–38 mm diameter			P or MDF	4

* Can be turned on a wood lathe or purchased from woodturning centres and craft shops.

Material key: P = pine

OTHER MATERIALS

- Nails; screws or wall anchors for mounting
- Woodworking adhesive
- Paint or lacquer

TOOLS

- Hand saw or mitre drop saw
- Portable electric drill
- Drill bit: 15 mm Forstner

Substitute other tools or equipment as desired. Additional common hand tools and clamps may be required.

Always observe the safety precautions in the owner's manual when using a tool or a piece of machinery.

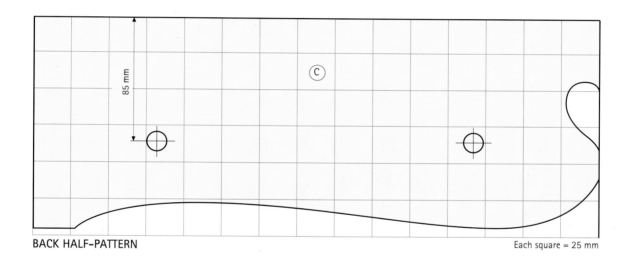

BACK HALF-PATTERN

Each square = 25 mm

other side. Then cut the shape out using a jigsaw.

FINISHING

8 Sand the edges of the back. Measure down 85 mm from the top edge of the back and draw a line along the face. Mark the positions of the shaker pegs (D) on this line, spaced 225 mm apart. Drill the peg holes, using the appropriate Forstner bit.

9 Sand all components. Glue and nail the back and shelf supports together using 38 mm long panel pins. Fix the top onto the frame, keeping it flush at the back.

10 Glue the shaker pegs into their holes. Remove any excess adhesive with a damp rag. When the adhesive has dried, apply a finish.

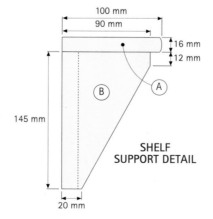

SHELF
SUPPORT DETAIL

11 Mount the shelf and pegboard onto the wall by inserting 8 g x 45 mm screws through the back board into wall studs or by using an appropriate wall anchor.

PADDLE-POP-STICK JOINERY

A packet of Paddle Pop sticks (usually made of soft timber such as poplar) is handy to have in the workshop. Use the sticks as shims when you need thin packers or when joints are loose. Simply cut a piece the right size, apply adhesive to both faces and insert it. Paddle Pop sticks are soft enough to adhere to the bottom of uneven furniture legs without damaging the floor, make good stirrers for adhesives and small paint cans and are useful to scrape off unwanted adhesive.

New Table from the Past

The warmth and charm of old furniture pieces don't usually come cheaply. This dining table, built from recycled oregon, can, however, be made for a fraction of the cost of antique or reproduction pieces.

Built to seat six, this durable, recycled oregon table is a welcome addition to any dining area.

TIMBER

| PART | FINISHED SIZE IN MM | | | MATERIAL | QUANTITY |
	W	T	L		
A top	156	26	1790	RO	5
B legs	90	90	740	RO	4
C long sides	90	30	1460	RO	2
D short sides	90	30	575	RO	2
E corner braces	70	30	250	RO	4
F battens	70	30	525	RO	3

Material key: RO = recycled oregon

OTHER MATERIALS

- PVA woodworking adhesive
- Nails
- 8 g x 75 mm screws
- 40 mm screws
- Satin polyurethane

TOOLS

- Pincers
- Drill
- Drill bits: 3 mm, 5 mm, spade bit
- Jigsaw
- Orbital sander
- Electric planer
- Circular rip saw
- Drop mitre saw
- Five 900 mm sash clamps
- Router
- Router bit: ovalo cutter

Substitute other tools or equipment as desired. Additional common hand tools and clamps may be required.

Always observe the safety precautions in the owner's manual when using a tool or a piece of machinery.

MAKING THE TABLE TOP

The timber thicknesses shown are not standard sizes but are obtained after recycled timber has been cleaned up with the electric planer.

You should be able to buy the recycled oregon used for this project from a demolition yard. Look for pieces with straight grain lines that are close together. Don't reject pieces with holes formed by old nails (the holes will add interest). Allow to lose at least a couple of millimetres off all faces of the timber.

1 Carefully take all the nails out of the timber, then clean it up with the electric sander. Set the blade for a 1 mm cut and do single passes until the timber faces are clean and square.

2 Cut five matching pieces of 156 x 26 mm oregon, 1790 mm long for the table top (A).

3 Lay the pieces flat on a work bench, edge to edge, with the best face of each piece facing up. Take a look at the ends of each piece to determine the positions of the growth rings. Then place the boards so that the growth rings alternate. That is, one piece will have rings facing up, then one will have rings facing down (see the Growth Rings diagram, right). This will help to prevent the table top from cupping and will ensure that it remains flat when it is glued and fixed in position.

4 Check that each board fits tightly up against the one next to it. Plane or sand the edges if required.

5 Drive four nails with a maximum gauge of 2 mm into one edge of each joined board. With a pair of pincers, cut the heads from all the nails, leaving approximately 5 to 10 mm of the nail protruding. (The nails should have sharp end points, which will be pushed onto the adjoining boards.)

6 Apply PVA woodworking adhesive to the edges of each of the joints. Clamp all the boards together, using sash clamps. Make sure that all the joints pull up tightly together and that there are no gaps. Remove the excess adhesive with a wet rag.

7 To make sure that the top pieces will remain flat, attach a stout piece of timber across the pieces at each end of the top with a quick-action clamp. Leave the pieces clamped this way overnight, until the adhesive has dried.

FORMING THE LEGS OF THE TABLE

8 Cut four pieces 90 x 90 mm oregon, 740 mm long for the legs (B). Lay a leg on the workbench and mark 150 mm from the top (this part of the leg (part 1) will not be tapered). Divide the remainder of the leg into three equal parts (parts 2, 3 and 4).

9 Working on one leg face at a time, set a plane at 2 mm and do a single pass from part 3 to 4 (the blade should be lined up at the part 3 mark to start). Next do a pass from 2 to 4 and finally a pass from 1 to 4. One face of the leg should now be tapered. Taper the remaining faces of the leg and the faces of the other three legs.

10 To form the feet, place a leg on the workbench and nail a block to the bench at the foot of the leg. Set the plane at 3 mm and on one face do a single pass from part 1 to the point where the front of the plane is stopped by the block. Repeat this procedure for the remaining faces and the other legs.

GROWTH RINGS

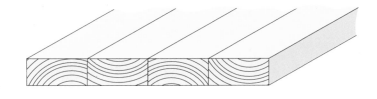

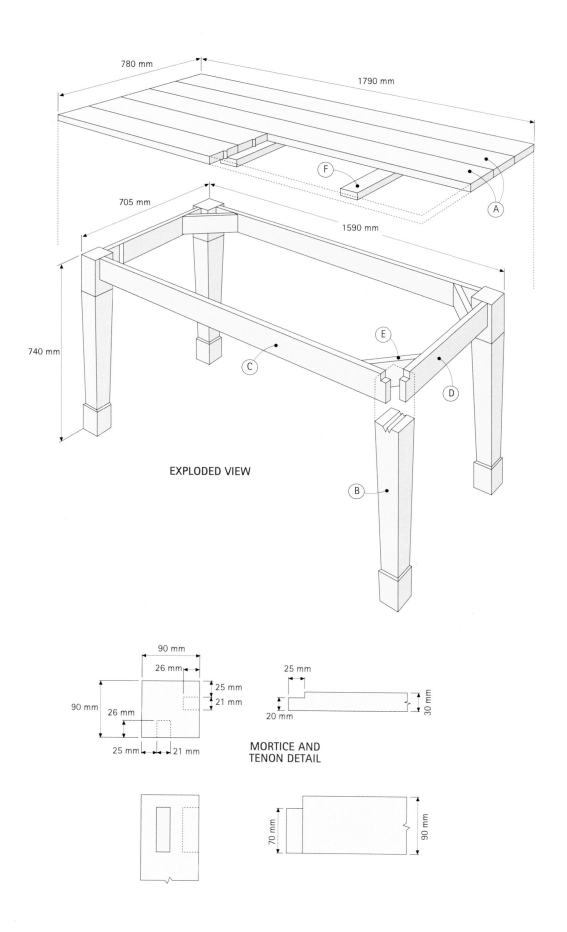

780 mm

1790 mm

F

A

705 mm

1590 mm

740 mm

C

E

D

B

EXPLODED VIEW

90 mm

26 mm

25 mm

21 mm

90 mm

26 mm

25 mm

21 mm

25 mm

20 mm

30 mm

MORTICE AND TENON DETAIL

70 mm

90 mm

11 Use a sander to remove any marks left by the planer and finish-sand the tapers.

ATTACHING THE SIDE RAILS

12 Cut two pieces of 90 x 30 maple, 1460 long for the long side rails (C). Referring to the Mortise and Tenon Detail diagram (see page 44), cut a tenon 25 mm long on each end with a hand saw.

13 Cut two pieces of 90 x 30 mm oregon 575 mm long, for the short side rails (D). Following the same procedure as for the long side rails, form a tenon 25 mm long on each end.

14 Mark out the mortise on the two inside edges of your table legs (see the Mortise and Tenon Detail diagram, page 44), ensuring that the top edges of the rails are flush with the end of each leg.

15 Using a spade bit, drill out the excess from the mortise. Then square up the edges of the mortise with a 20 mm chisel.

16 Test fit each tenon by placing it in the corresponding mortise, adjusting either the mortise or tenon to obtain a snug fit.

17 Glue the short and then the long side rails into the legs by applying adhesive to the tenon and pulling the joints together with the sash clamps. While still in the clamps, insert two 8 g x 75 mm screws through the inside of each leg to hold the joint.

ATTACHING THE CORNER BRACES TO THE RAILS

18 Check that the completed frame is square. Cut four pieces of 70 x 30 mm oregon 250 mm long for the corner braces (E).

19 Skew-screw the braces in position by inserting two screws at the end of each brace through the edges into the perimeter frame.

FIXING THE BATTENS TO THE TOP OF THE TABLE

20 Remove the top from the clamps and lay it upside down on the bench. Cut two battens (F), each 525 mm long, from 70 x 30 mm oregon.

21 Measure 550 mm in from each end of the table top and screw-fix each batten in place 92 mm in from the table edge.

22 Lift the table frame onto the top and centre it. At 200 mm intervals, drill 5 mm clearance holes through the inside of the rails at a skew angle and fix the top into position using 40 mm screws.

FINISHING

23 Turn the table right side up and mark a 70 mm radius curve at each corner. Cut the rounds with a jigsaw and sand smooth (see the step 23 illustration, below).

24 Place a 10 mm ovalo cutter in the router and mould the edges of the table top.

25 Sand the whole unit with an orbital sander. Don't fill the holes and dents (these marks add to the table's rustic appeal). Apply two to three coats of satin polyurethane.

LEG DETAIL

STEP 23   Mark a 70 mm radius curve at each corner. Cut the curve with a jigsaw and sand the corner smooth.

Knife Block

Our combined knife block and kitchen utensil holder can be built in just a few hours, and it is an ideal piece for someone learning to use electric tools. A jigsaw, an electric plane and an electric drill were used to make the block featured.

ASSEMBLING THE BASE, THE BACK, THE SIDES AND THE DIVIDERS

1 Cut a piece of 243 x 25 mm oregon, 255 mm long for the base (A). Referring to the Side View diagram (see page 47), make a template for the sides on a piece of cardboard or hardboard. (You could use a small tin base to draw the curves.) Cut the template out with a jigsaw and sand it smooth. Cut two pieces of 243 x 25 mm oregon, 260 mm long for the sides (B). Use the template to transfer the shape to the side pieces. Cut the sides out with a jigsaw, then sand them smooth by hand or with a small drum sander.

2 Cut the back (C), the divider (D) and the knife dividers (E) to size (see the Timber list, page 47). Then, using a 5 mm spacer, glue each knife divider onto the back and secure with 38 mm long panel pins. Make sure that both of the outside dividers are flush with the outside edge of the back.

3 Glue and nail the divider (D) over the face of the knife dividers to form the knife sheath. Wipe off any excess glue as you go with a damp rag. Assemble the sides and the knife sheath by drilling 3.5 mm clearance holes through the sides and then countersinking them using a drill fitted with a 10 mm dowel bit. Screw the sides and the sheath together with 6 g x 38 mm screws. Carve 10 mm plug pieces from square sections of timber, apply a little glue, then hammer the plugs into the screw holes to cover the holes. Sand any excess from each plug until it is flush.

MAKING THE FRONT PANEL AND RAILS

4 Cut the front panel (F), top rail (G) and bottom rail (H) to size (see the Timber list, page 47). Using a hand plane or a router with a round-over bit, round over one top edge of the top rail.

The knife block featured was made from recycled oregon, but any new or used pieces of softwood timber can be used.

TIMBER

PART	FINISHED SIZE IN MM			MATERIAL	QUANTITY
	W	T	L		
A base	243	25	255	RO	1
B sides	243	25	260	RO	2
C back	202	25	260	RO	1
D divider	205	25	260	RO	1
E knife dividers	45	25	260	RO	7
F front panel	205	25	115	RO	1
G top rail	50	25	205	RO	1
H bottom rail	50	25	205	RO	1
I feet	30	6	30	HB	4

Material key: RO = recycled oregon, HB = hardboard (Masonite)

OTHER MATERIALS

- Woodworking adhesive
- 38 mm panel pins
- 6 g x 38 mm screws
- 45 mm panel pins
- 16 mm panel pins
- Wood filler
- Polyurethane

TOOLS

- Jigsaw
- Electric plane
- Electric drill
- Drill bit: 10 mm dowel
- Small drum sander
- Router
- Router bit: chamfer

Substitute other tools or equipment as desired. Additional common hand tools and clamps may be required.

Always observe the safety precautions in the owner's manual when using a tool or a piece of machinery.

5 Glue and nail the front panel and base into position, using 45 mm panel pins.

6 Apply a small bead of glue to the bottom edge of the bottom rail and push it down into position, 50 mm in from the front panel. Secure it in position with two 45 mm panel pins.

7 Cut a 6 mm, 45-degree chamfer along the top edges of the sides using a router fitted with a chamfer bit. Stop chamfering the inside edge at the front panel and the outside edge about half-way down the front.

8 Place adhesive on the ends of the top rail and slide it in position directly above the bottom rail and the lower edge (it should be 10 mm down from the front). Secure the rail in place by inserting two 45 mm panel pins through each side.

FINISHING

9 Cut four pieces of 6 mm Masonite to form 30 x 30 mm triangles for the feet of the block (I). Glue and secure the feet, one in each corner of the base, using 16 mm panel pins.

10 Punch each of the nails and fill the holes with wood filler. Sand the entire block smooth, then apply two coats of polyurethane.

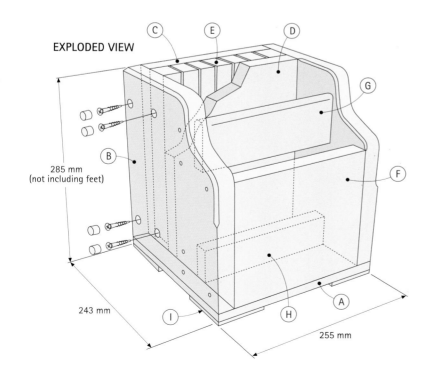

EXPLODED VIEW

285 mm (not including feet)

243 mm

255 mm

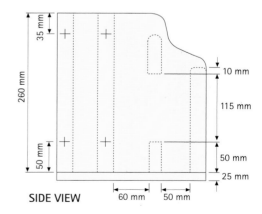

SIDE VIEW

35 mm
260 mm
50 mm
10 mm
115 mm
50 mm
25 mm
60 mm
50 mm

Flight School Birdhouse

This charming house will attract plenty of small nesting birds. When it's time for a spring clean, you will enjoy the convenience of the removable floor.

Use the template to paint the charming flight school facade on the birdhouse or simply finish it with natural, contrasting colours.

TIMBER

| PART | FINISHED SIZE IN MM | | | | |
	W	T	L	MATERIAL	QUANTITY
A* front/back	165	19	263	P	2
B sides	167	19	152	P	2
C* floor	106	19	114	P	1
D* roof	181	19	254	P	2
E cap	25	25	254	OCM	1

Initially cut parts marked with an * oversized, then trim them to the finished size according to the step-by-step instructions.

Material key: P = pine, OCM = outside corner moulding

OTHER MATERIALS

- 45 mm panel pins
- Woodworking adhesive; carbon paper
- Chain or wire for hanging; 6 mm screw eyes

TOOLS

- Table saw
- Band saw
- Belt sander
- Portable drill
- Drill press
- Drill bits: 2.5 mm, 3 mm
- Forstner bits: 10 mm, 30 mm
- Orbital sander

Substitute other tools or equipment as desired. Additional common hand tools and clamps may be required.

Always observe the safety precautions in the owner's manual when using a tool or a piece of machinery.

CUTTING OUT THE PARTS

1 Rip and cross-cut two pieces of 19 mm pine to 176 x 267 mm long for the front and back blanks (A). (This project only requires a small amount of wood, so you may be able to use leftover timber.)

2 Stack the front and back blanks face-to-face, using double-sided tape. Then draw diagonal lines to mark the centreline on the face of the front piece.

3 Photocopy or make a carbon copy of the Full-sized Front Pattern (see page 50). Cut out the pattern, leaving a 6 to 12 mm margin around all sides. Adhere your copy to the front piece with spray adhesive, aligning the pattern's centreline with the centreline you marked on the front blank.

4 Referring to the Step 4 illustration below, band saw the front and back pieces to shape, cutting just outside the pattern line. Then, using a stationary belt sander, sand each cut edge smooth to the line.

5 To make the sides, from 19 mm pine cross-cut a piece 184 x 330 mm long (B).

6 Referring to the Step 6 illustration below, tilt your saw blade to cut a 33-degree bevel. (Use an adjustable triangle to set the blade angle.) Bevel-rip one edge of the piece. Return the saw blade to vertical, lock the fence 167 mm from the inside face of the blade, place the bevelled edge of your piece against the fence and make the cut. Cross-cut two 152 mm long sides from the piece.

7 To make the birdhouse floor (C), select a piece of 19 mm pine that is oversized, at least 127 x 305 mm long, to make cutting safer. Tilt the saw blade to 12 degrees from perpendicular. Bevel-rip one edge of the 305 mm long piece. Then bevel-rip the other edge, cutting it to a final width of 106 mm. Make sure you check the direction of the bevel on each edge before making any cuts. Then cross-cut a 114 mm long floor piece.

8 For the birdhouse roof (D), select a piece of 19 mm timber that is at least 184 x 525 mm long. Tilt your saw blade to 45 degrees from perpendicular and bevel-cut one edge on the piece. Then return the saw blade to perpendicular and set the saw fence 181 mm from the inside of the saw blade. Place the bevelled edge of the roof piece against the rip fence and rip it to width. Cross-cut two 254 mm lengths from the piece.

9 For the roof cap (E), cross-cut a 254 mm length of 25 mm outside corner moulding. (Moulding is available at hardware stores. If you prefer to make your own cap, use a 305 mm length of 25 mm x 25 mm pine.)

10 Then, referring to the Cap Detail diagram (see page 51), saw the cap piece and cross-cut the piece to the final length.

ASSEMBLING AND PAINTING

11 Referring to the Exploded View diagram (see page 51), drill the 6 mm vent holes through the floor, sides and the front and back pieces. Then separate the front and back pieces and bore the 30 mm diameter entry hole through the front piece. Remove the pattern and finish-sand all the pieces.

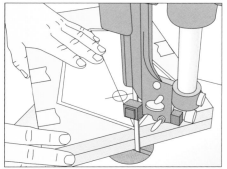

STEP 4   Cutting just outside the pattern line, band saw the front and back pieces to shape.

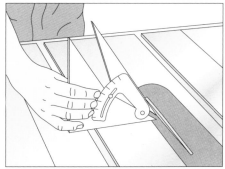

STEP 6   Use an adjustable triangle to set the angle for the bevel in the side pieces.

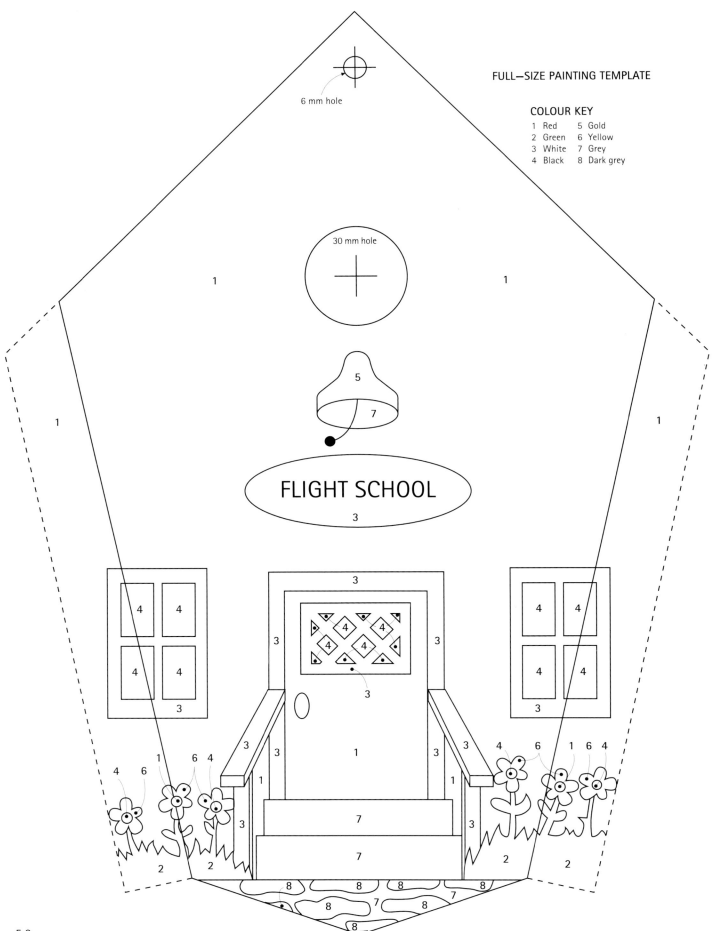

6 mm hole

FULL–SIZE PAINTING TEMPLATE

COLOUR KEY
1 Red   5 Gold
2 Green   6 Yellow
3 White   7 Grey
4 Black   8 Dark grey

30 mm hole

FLIGHT SCHOOL

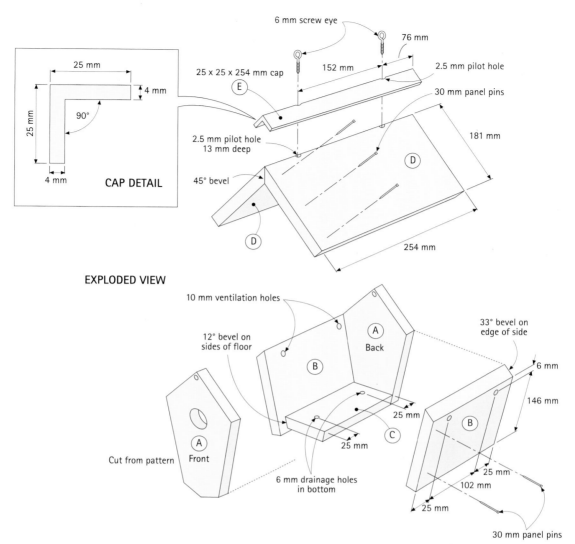

CAP DETAIL

EXPLODED VIEW

12 Using waterproof adhesive and 45 mm panel pins, glue and nail the sides to the front and back. Then glue and nail the two roof pieces together. Position the roof so that it is centred on the house and glue and nail it to the front and back. Punch all nails below the surface. Glue the cap to the roof.

13 Place the floor piece inside the house and turn it so that it falls and wedges in place between the sides and the front and back. Do not glue or nail the bottom. Sized correctly, it should fit snugly in place and be easy to remove for cleaning.

14 Finish your house as you wish. If you would like your birdhouse to look like the model in the photograph, using carbon paper, transfer the Full-size Painting Template (see page 50) onto the front, sides and back. Use the colour scheme on page 50 to paint the Flight School design or create your scheme. If

you prefer a simple paint job, use an exterior flat paint and neutral colours such as grey, green or light brown. If you finish the outside, let the application weather outdoors for about a month before moving it to a permanent location. If you leave your house unfinished, the wood should eventually weather to a natural grey. If you feel the birdhouse needs additional protection, use exterior-grade wood stains and wood preservatives. Do not paint or finish the interior of your birdhouse.

INSTALLING THE BIRDHOUSE

15 To hang your birdhouse, drill 25 mm pilot holes through the cap and 13 mm deep into the roof (see the Exploded View diagram, above). Turn 6 mm screw eyes into the holes and attach chains or wires to the screw eyes. If you prefer to mount the birdhouse on a post or a tree, screw a 101-wide mounting board to the back.

TIPS TO ATTRACT BIRDS

• A house this size will appeal to small nesters. To attract larger birds, increase the floor area, deepen the cavity and enlarge the entry hole.

• Suspend the house from two lines, for greater stability. Make sure that it is hung at a height desirable to the type of bird you would like to attract.

• Orient the house so that the entry hole faces away from prevailing winds and it is shaded from direct sun during the hottest part of the day.

• Clean the house at the end of each brooding period or when undesirable birds move in.

Shaker-style Buffet

This contemporary version of a Shaker buffet is made from European oak over a lightweight plywood frame. This gives the buffet a solid timber appearance without too much expense and labour. The modern base suits today's decor.

The clean lines of the cabinet and the natural beauty of the European oak are enhanced by using a clear finish.

ASSEMBLING THE CABINET

1 From 19 mm European oak plywood, rip and crosscut the cabinet top (A) to 451 x 1473 mm long, the bottom (B) to 425 x 1948 mm long, the two end panels (C) to 432 x 803 mm long, the two fixed shelves (D) to 425 x 721 mm long, and divider (E) to 425 x 721 mm long (see the Cutting diagram, page 57).

2 Using a table saw and a dado blade, cut or rout the rebates and trenches in pieces A, B, C and E (see the Exploded View Diagram, page 56, and Part View diagram, page 53).

3 Dry-clamp the pieces to check the fit, and trim them, if necessary. Then glue and clamp the pieces, checking for square.

4 Measure the opening and cut the 6 mm plywood back (F) to size (see the Cutting diagram, page 57).

5 Cut the centre support (G) to size (see the Timber list, page 54). Then mark and cut a notch along the bottom edge (see the Exploded View diagram, page 56). Glue it in place directly under the divider (E).

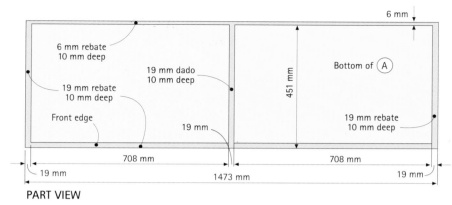

PART VIEW

6 mm rebate 10 mm deep

19 mm dado 10 mm deep

19 mm rebate 10 mm deep

Front edge

19 mm

451 mm

Bottom of (A)

19 mm rebate 10 mm deep

6 mm

708 mm

708 mm

19 mm

1473 mm

19 mm

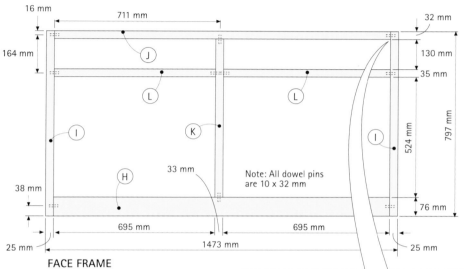

FACE FRAME

16 mm

711 mm

32 mm

164 mm

J

130 mm

L

L

35 mm

I

K

I

797 mm

524 mm

H

33 mm

Note: All dowel pins are 10 x 32 mm

38 mm

76 mm

695 mm

695 mm

25 mm

1473 mm

25 mm

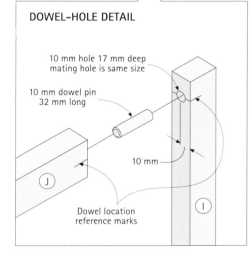

DOWEL-HOLE DETAIL

10 mm hole 17 mm deep mating hole is same size

10 mm dowel pin 32 mm long

10 mm

J

Dowel location reference marks

I

ADDING THE FACE FRAME

6 From solid 19 mm European oak timber, cut the bottom rail (H), stiles (I), top rail (J), mullion (K) and centre rails (L) (see the Timber list, page 54, and Cutting diagram, page 57).

7 Dry-clamp the face frame together. Measure the length and width of the clamped-up face frame and compare to that of the assembled cabinet. You should find that they are the same. The bottom of the face frame sits 6 mm above the ends (C) (see the Side Section diagram, page 56). Referring to the Face Frame diagram and the Dowel-hole Detail diagram (see above), mark the dowel-hole location centrelines across each joint. Remove the clamps.

8 Using a dowelling jig, drill 10 mm holes 17 mm deep for the dowel pins where marked.

9 Glue, dowel and clamp the frame, checking for square and twist. Allow the adhesive to dry, then remove the clamps and excess glue and sand the front and back of the face frame smooth.

10 Referring to the Step 10 illustration, glue and clamp the face frame to the cabinet.

MAKING THE TRIM, THE GUIDE PARTS AND THE DRAWERS

11 Cut a piece of 82 x 19 mm thick European oak, 1550 mm long for the front trim pieces (M, O), and two pieces 82 mm wide and 505 mm long for the side trim pieces (N, P).

12 Following the sequence outlined on the Forming the Trim diagram (see page 56), cut the decorative front trim pieces (M, O) from the 1550 mm long piece, and the side trim pieces (N, P) from the 508 mm long pieces. (It is a good idea to test each cut first on a piece of scrap timber.) Then mitre-cut the front and side trim pieces to length.

13 Mark a notch on the bottom of the front trim piece (M) (see the Trim Detail on the Exploded View diagram, page 56). Then, with a jigsaw, cutting just outside the marked line, cut the notch with its angled ends to shape.

14 Glue and clamp the trim pieces to the cabinet. The front trim piece should sit 6 mm below the bottom edge of the face-frame member (H) and be flush

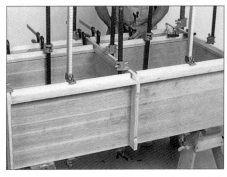

STEP 10 Rest the buffet on its back while gluing and clamping the face frame to the unit.

TIMBER

PART	W	T	L	MATERIAL	QUANTITY
	FINISHED SIZE IN MM				
CABINET					
A top	451	19	1473	EOP	1
B bottom	426	19	1448	EOP	1
C end panels	432	19	803	EOP	2
D fixed shelves	426	19	721	EOP	2
E divider	426	19	721	EOP	1
F back	740	6	1454	EOP	1
G centre support	64	19	432	EO	1
FACE FRAME					
H bottom rail	76	19	1422	EO	1
I stiles	25	19	797	EO	2
J top rail	32	19	1422	EO	1
K mullion	33	19	689	EO	1
L centre rails	35	19	695	EO	2
TRIM					
M* bottom front	57	19	1512	EO	1
N* bottom sides	57	19	470	EO	2
O* top front	19	19	1512	EO	1
P* top sides	19	19	470	EO	2
DRAWERS AND GUIDES					
Q kickers	22	19	426	EO	2
R runners	6	19	426	EO	4
S fronts	143	19	708	EO	2
T sides	121	13	432	EO	4
U backs	105	13	663	EO	2
V bottoms	403	6	663	EOP	2
DOORS					
W stiles	51	19	537	EO	8
X rails	51	19	276	EO	8
Y* panels	274	13	460	EEO	4
SHELVES					
Z shelves	400	19	706	EOP	2
AA fronts	10	19	706	EO	2
MOUNTING BLOCKS					
BB blocks	38	16	127	EO	2

Initially cut parts marked with an * oversized, then trim them to the finished size according to the step-by-step instructions.

Material key: EOP = European oak plywood, EO = European oak, EEO = edge-joined European oak

OTHER MATERIALS

- 6 g x 19 mm flathead wood screws
- 10 x 32 mm dowel pins
- 25 mm brads
- Eight 10 x 50 mm long inset hinges
- Woodworking adhesive
- Shelf clips
- Four magnetic catches with strike plates
- Two 30 mm knobs and four 22 mm knobs
- Finish

TOOLS

- Table saw
- Dado blade or dado set
- Router
- Router bit: 6 mm round-over
- Drill
- Drill bits: 1.5 mm, 2 mm, 6 mm, 10 mm
- Orbital sander

Substitute other tools and equipment as desired. Additional common hand tools and clamps may be required to complete the project.

Always observe the safety precautions in the owner's manual when using a tool or piece of machinery.

16 Cut the two drawer fronts (S) to size from 19 mm European oak (see the Cutting Diagram, page 57). (To preserve the grain pattern, cut them from one board, end to end.)

17 From 13 mm European oak, cut the drawer sides (T) and backs (U) to size. Cut the drawer bottoms (V) to size from 6 mm European oak plywood.

18 Referring to the Drawer diagram (see page 55), cut the rebates, grooves and trenches in the drawer parts.

19 Dry-clamp each drawer to check the fit. The bottom edge of the drawer front sits 10 mm lower than the bottom edge of the sides.

20 Locate the centrepoints on each drawer side, snip the head off a 25 mm brad and use the brad as a bit to drill pilot holes. Glue and nail the drawers, checking for square.

21 Mark the centrepoints for the pulls. Drill 10 mm holes 13 mm deep, centred, on each drawer front.

CONSTRUCTING THE DOORS

22 Cut the stiles (W) and rails (X) to size. Referring to the Tenon and Groove Detail on the Door Diagram (see page 55), cut or rout a 6 mm groove 13 mm deep along one edge of each rail and stile. Then cut a tenon 13 mm long on each end of the rails.

with the bottom edge of the cabinet side pieces (C) (see the Side Section diagram, page 56).

15 Cut the kickers (Q) and runners (R) to size (see the Timber list, above), Clamp and glue them to the cabinet.

23 Cut four pieces of 13 mm European oak to 276 x 460 mm for the panels (Y) by edge-joining narrower timber. Cut 19 mm rebates 6 mm deep along the front edges of each panel (see the Door diagram, below).

24 Test-fit the door pieces. The panel should be 1.5 mm undersized in each direction to allow it to expand. Glue and clamp the stiles, rails and panel for each door. Allow the panel to float inside the frame without glue.

25 Referring to the Hinge Detail diagram, cut or rout 10 mm rebates 10 mm deep along the back outside edges of the door (except the edge without the hinge).

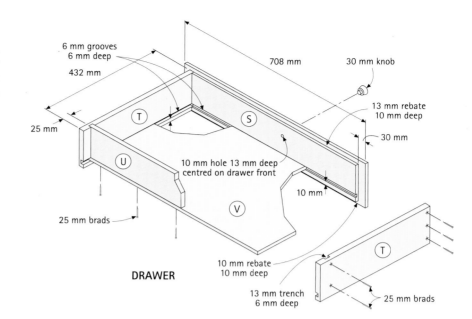

DRAWER

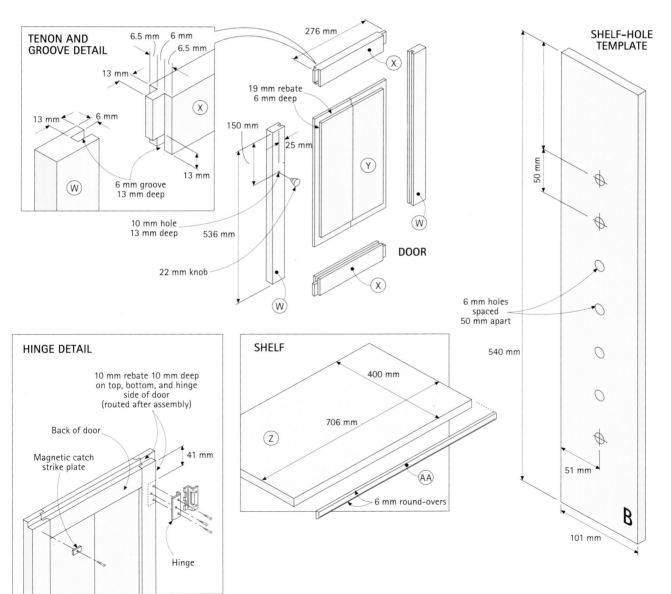

TENON AND GROOVE DETAIL

DOOR

SHELF-HOLE TEMPLATE

HINGE DETAIL

SHELF

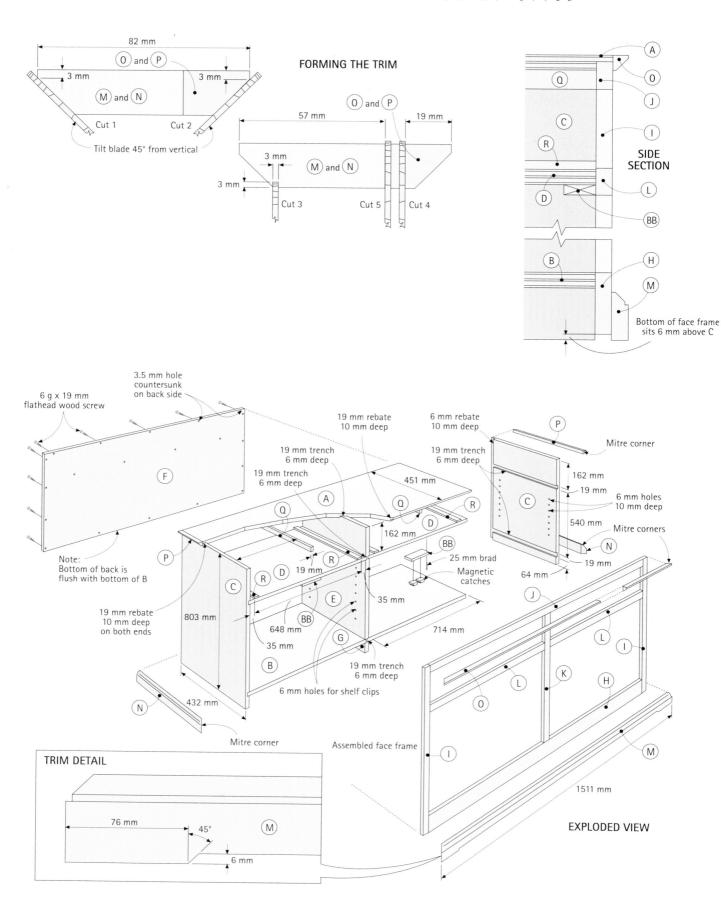

FORMING THE TRIM

82 mm

O and P

3 mm

3 mm

M and N

Cut 1

Cut 2

Tilt blade 45° from vertical

57 mm

19 mm

O and P

3 mm

M and N

3 mm

Cut 3

Cut 5

Cut 4

SIDE SECTION

A

O

Q

J

C

I

R

D

L

BB

B

H

M

Bottom of face frame sits 6 mm above C

6 g x 19 mm flathead wood screw

3.5 mm hole countersunk on back side

19 mm rebate 10 mm deep

6 mm rebate 10 mm deep

19 mm trench 6 mm deep

19 mm trench 6 mm deep

451 mm

19 mm trench 6 mm deep

F

Q

A

Q

R

P

C

R

D

162 mm

D

19 mm

BB

6 mm holes 10 mm deep

540 mm

P

Mitre corner

162 mm

19 mm

C

N

Mitre corners

19 mm

25 mm brad

64 mm

Magnetic catches

Note:
Bottom of back is flush with bottom of B

R

E

35 mm

J

19 mm rebate 10 mm deep on both ends

803 mm

BB

648 mm

G

714 mm

L

I

35 mm

O

L

K

H

B

19 mm trench 6 mm deep

6 mm holes for shelf clips

Assembled face frame

I

M

N

432 mm

Mitre corner

1511 mm

TRIM DETAIL

76 mm

45°

M

6 mm

EXPLODED VIEW

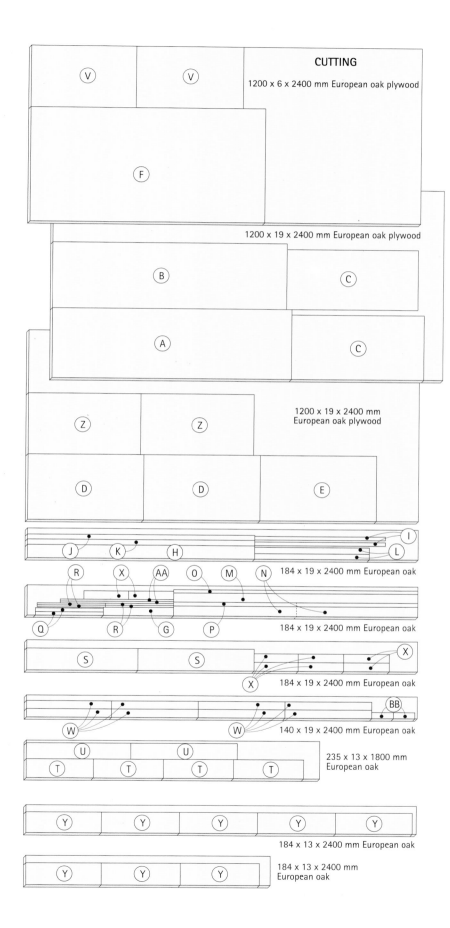

CUTTING

1200 x 6 x 2400 mm European oak plywood

1200 x 19 x 2400 mm European oak plywood

1200 x 19 x 2400 mm
European oak plywood

184 x 19 x 2400 mm European oak

184 x 19 x 2400 mm European oak

184 x 19 x 2400 mm European oak

140 x 19 x 2400 mm European oak

235 x 13 x 1800 mm
European oak

184 x 13 x 2400 mm European oak

184 x 13 x 2400 mm
European oak

MAKING THE SHELVES

26 Cut the shelves (Z) and shelf fronts (AA) to size. Glue the fronts to the shelves with the top surfaces and ends flush.

27 Referring to the Shelf diagram (see page 55), rout a 6 mm round-over along the top and bottom outside edges of each attached front.

ADDING THE SHELVES

28 Cut a scrap of tempered hardboard to 101 x 540 mm to use as a hole template. Mark a centreline and drill 6 mm holes (see the Shelf-hole Template diagram, page 55). Place the letter 'B' (for bottom) on the bottom end of your template. When drilling the shelf holes, keep this mark to the bottom to ensure that each hole remains the same distance from the bottom edge.

29 Using the template on the inside of the cabinet, drill the 6 mm shelf-clip holes 10 mm deep where shown on the Exploded View diagram. (Use a stop on the drill bit to prevent drilling through the cabinet sides.)

ADDING THE HARDWARE AND THE FINISH

30 Referring to the Hinge Detail diagram on the Door Diagram (page 55), add the hinges to the doors. Then with the top and bottom edges flush and an even gap between each pair of doors, fasten the hinged doors to the cabinet.

31 Cut the mounting blocks (BB) to size and glue and brad them to the bottom side of the shelves (D). Add the magnetic catches to the mounting blocks and fasten the strikes to the door backs. Mark the centrepoints and drill the holes for the pull knobs in the doors.

32 Remove the hardware. Sand the cabinet, drawers and doors smooth. Add the finish to all parts including the knobs, being careful not to get finish in the holes for the knobs. Attach the hardware and glue the knobs in place.

Heirloom Tree Ornaments

These traditional Christmas decorations, turned on a lathe, are handsome enough for just about any tree.

Decorate the ornaments with bright, festive colours for added sparkle.

TURNING THE TIMBER

1 Cut a piece of kauri pine 44 mm square and 152 mm long for each decoration (A). Find the centre on one end, drill a pilot hole there and mount the timber onto a screw centre. To avoid hitting the centre when turning, leave a small waste block next to the faceplate. If you do not have a screw centre, turn the ornament between centres with the top (screw-eyed end) against the tailstock. Turn the larger sections first and use the skew chisel to cut the base of the turning last. Be careful not to allow the turning to fly out of the lathe as the chisel cuts through. The tailstock centre mark will become the point of insertion for the screw-eyes.

2 Set a tool rest in position and using a 25 mm gouge, with the lathe set on a slow speed (about 600 rpm) turn the entire length of the kauri to produce a 38 mm diameter cylinder.

3 Using carbon paper, trace a copy of the first of the Full-size Half-patterns (see page 59) along one edge of piece of posterboard. Hold this up to the cylinder, turn on the lathe and transfer all of the lines to the turning piece of timber with a pencil.

4 Using the pencil marks you have made as guides, use a 13 mm gouge to reduce the bottom portion of the turning (the portion furthest away from the headstock) to 10 mm in diameter. With a 13 mm chisel, cut the half beads and full beads on the end. To do this, hold the chisel between a finger and thumb, with the cutting edge almost flat. Rotate your wrist, rolling the chisel over and forward in the same movement. This will allow the corner of the chisel to cut the round bead.

5 Cut each of the larger convex curves with the 13 mm gouge or skew chisel. Start at the top of each

TIMBER

PART	FINISHED SIZE IN MM			MATERIAL	QUANTITY
	W	T	L		
A ornaments	44	44	152	KP	3

Material key: KP = kauri pine

OTHER MATERIALS

- Carbon paper
- 80-grit, 120-grit sandpaper; water-based acrylic paint
- Screw eyes

TOOLS

- Lathe
- Screw drive centre
- 25 mm roughing gouge
- 10 mm, 13 mm spindle gouges
- 13 mm skew chisel

Substitute other tools or equipment as desired.

Always observe the safety precautions in the owner's manual when using a tool or a piece of machinery.

FULL-SIZE HALF PATTERNS

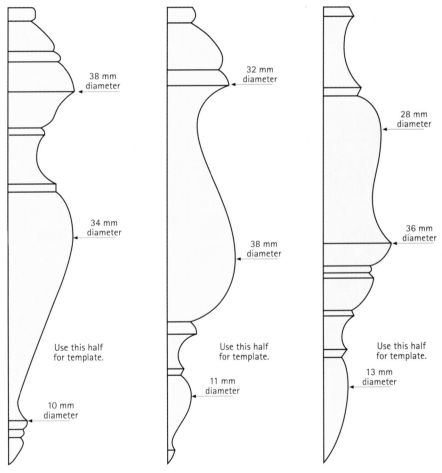

38 mm diameter

34 mm diameter

Use this half for template.

10 mm diameter

32 mm diameter

38 mm diameter

Use this half for template.

11 mm diameter

28 mm diameter

36 mm diameter

Use this half for template.

13 mm diameter

shape (the larger diameter) and work down to the smaller diameter. Cut the concave shapes using a 13 mm gouge for the larger curves and a 10 mm gouge for the smaller concave shapes. Again, start at the top of the shape, however this time hold the hollow of the gouge vertical. Use the point of the gouge to cut, using a rolling movement to gradually cut deeper into the timber and along the hollow of the shape, until you obtain the shape that is desired.

6 Clean the sharp corners of each fillet using the skew chisel. Cut the large tapered shape with a 13 mm skew chisel, joining up the beads and hollows.

FINISHING

7 Clean each ornament with sandpaper, starting with 80 grit paper and finishing off with 120 grit paper. Be careful not to sand off the sharp corners. Then use a stiff brush, with bristles about 6 mm long by 6 mm wide, and water-based acrylic paint the consistency of cream to paint each ornament while still on the lathe. The lathe should be running at about 600 rpm. Apply the paint heavily, just short of it flying off while being applied.

8 After the paint has dried, remove the ornament from the lathe and cut off the scrap end. Sand and paint the ends. Then insert a small screw eye for hanging.

STEP 5 Using a 13 mm gouge, cut the large tapers, working from the larger diameter down the grain to the smaller diameter.

STEP 7 Paint the ornament while it is turning on the lathe at about 600 rpm.

Shaker Oval Carrier

Re-live an earlier period in history by constructing this traditional Shaker carrier. The timber for its sides and handle is curved by applying hot water to it.

Thin timber is required for the carrier and handle sections. To obtain timber the correct width, plane or resaw thicker timber to size.

CONSTRUCTING THE BAND FORM

1 Cut four pieces of 19 mm thick pine to 230 x 150 mm long, for the band form (A) (You could also use two pieces 230 x 50 mm long.) Glue and clamp the pieces with the ends and edges flush.

2 Transfer the Full-size Band Form Pattern (see page 61) to the top piece of timber. Band saw the form to shape. Sand the form edges.

3 Referring to the Full-Size Band Form Pattern, mark the starting point reference line on the top surface of the band form.

FORMING THE SUPPORT AND THE SHAPERS

4 Build the support (B, C) (see the Pipe Support diagram and the Timber list, page 63). You will use this and a pipe clamp to clinch the tacks that hold the carrier together later.

5 To make the shapers (D), transfer the shaper outline from the full-size pattern onto two pieces of 19 mm pine 150 x 225 mm long. Tilt your band-saw table 10 degrees from horizontal. Band saw the two shapers to shape, cutting just outside the marked line (the entire line should still be visible when you have finished cutting). Referring to the Shaping the Carrier Band diagram (page 64), drill two 25 mm holes in each shaper.

MAKING THE CARRIER BAND

6 Cut a piece of 2 mm Victorian ash to 76 x 685 mm long for the band (E) (see the Cutting diagram, page 63).

7 Transfer the Full-size Band Form Pattern (page 61) with finger details and hole locations to one end of the band. Drill twelve 1.5 mm holes through the band where marked.

8 Referring to the Sanding the Taper diagram (see page 64), sand a 38 mm long taper on the end opposite the fingers.

9 Band saw the fingers to shape. Referring to the Full-size Band Pattern (see page 62), use a utility or hobby knife to bevel-cut the edges and ends of

each finger. (Bevel the insides of the fingers at 20 degrees and reduce the bevel to 10 degrees near the ends of the fingers.) Then finish forming the bevelled 'V' where the 20 degrees cuts meet. Bevel-cut the ends of the fingers.

10 Soak the band in hot water for 25 minutes. (You could do this in a plastic wallpaper water tray or in a bathtub.) Drain the water and immediately pour boiling water over the band and soak it for 1 minute. Working quickly, remove the band from the water and wrap it snugly

Filled with fruit, the oval basket makes a superb centre piece for a country-kitchen table.

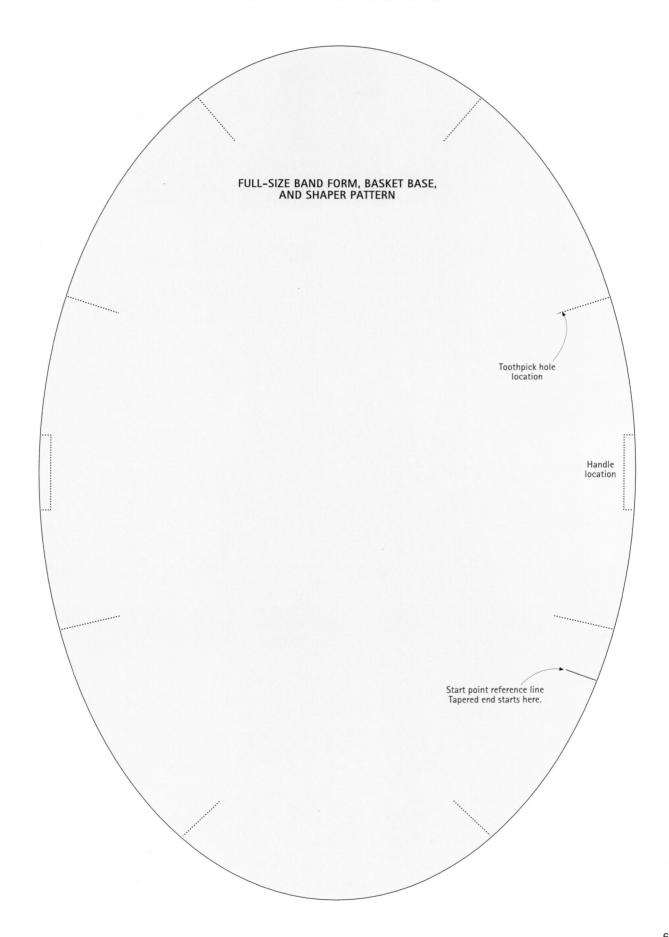

FULL-SIZE BAND FORM, BASKET BASE, AND SHAPER PATTERN

Toothpick hole
location

Handle
location

Start point reference line
Tapered end starts here.

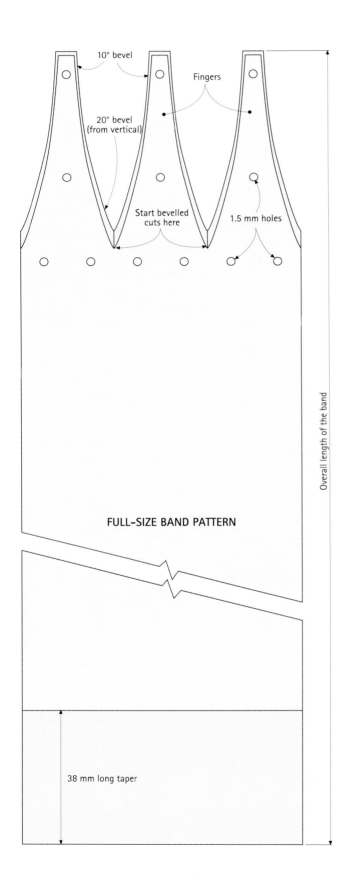

10° bevel

Fingers

20° bevel
(from vertical)

Start bevelled
cuts here

1.5 mm holes

Overall length of the band

FULL-SIZE BAND PATTERN

38 mm long taper

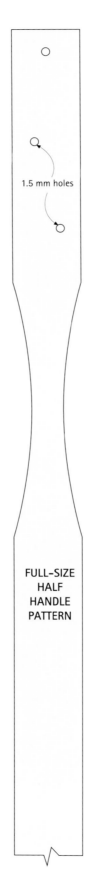

1.5 mm holes

1.5 mm holes

**FULL-SIZE
HALF
HANDLE
PATTERN**

around the form. Position the band so that the tapered end sits directly under the start-point reference line on the form and the bevelled edges on the fingers face out. To avoid splitting the band between the fingers, hold all three fingers until the tacks are secured in the following steps.

11 Referring to the Shaping the Carrier Band diagram (see page 64), lightly mark a reference line on the top-lapped edges of the band.

12 Insert a pipe clamp through the oval band, and place the pipe on the support. Lightly tighten the clamp to hold it to the support.

13 Hold the band with one hand so that the marked lines on the top edges align and the band edges are flush. Position the 1.5 mm holes in the band directly over the pipe.

14 Referring to the Step 14 illustration (see page 63), drive 12 mm copper tacks through the holes and against the pipe. The end of the tack will clinch against the pipe. Do not drive the tacks at an angle; as they will not clinch properly, causing the band to fit loosely.

15 Referring to the Shaping the Carrier Band diagram (see page 64), slip a shaper into each end of the band and let the band dry and cool on the shapers overnight.

SHAPING THE CARRIER BASE

16 Remove the shapers from the band, then sand the band interior smooth.

17 Resaw or plane a piece of 305 x 150 mm pine to 6 mm thick for the carrier base (F). Transfer the Full-size Basket Base Pattern to the carrier base piece (see page 61). Band saw the carrier base to shape, cutting about 3 mm outside the marked line.

18 Tilt the table on your disc sander 4 degrees from horizontal (or use a belt sander on a conversion stand). Bevel-sand to the line until the base fits snugly into the band and the bottom edge of the band is flush with the bottom edge of the base.

TIMBER

FINISHED SIZE IN MM

PART	W	T	L	MATERIAL	QUANTITY
A band form	150	19	230	P	4
B pipe support bottom	88	38	125	P	1
C pipe support sides	88	38	175	P	2
D shapers	150	19	225	P	2
E band	76	2	685	VA	1
F base	150	6	305	VA	1
G handle	19	3	470	VA	1

Material key: VA = Victorian ash, P = pine

OTHER MATERIALS

- 38 x 6 mm copper tacks
- 38 x 12 mm copper tacks
- Wood pegs

TOOLS

- Table saw
- Band saw
- Drill
- Drill bits: 1.5 mm, 2.5 mm, 25 mm
- Disc sander
- Belt sander
- Orbital sander

Substitute other tools or equipment as desired. Additional common hand tools and clamps may be required.

Always observe the safety precautions in the owner's manual when using a tool or a piece of machinery.

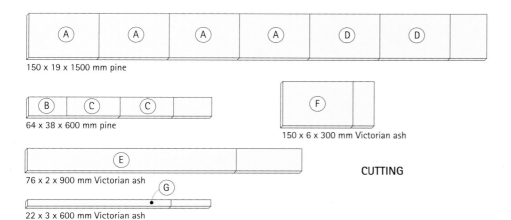

150 x 19 x 1500 mm pine

64 x 38 x 600 mm pine

150 x 6 x 300 mm Victorian ash

76 x 2 x 900 mm Victorian ash

22 x 3 x 600 mm Victorian ash

CUTTING

BAND FORM

Use full-size pattern for shape.

Start point reference line

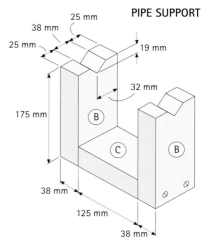

PIPE SUPPORT

25 mm
38 mm
25 mm
19 mm
32 mm
175 mm
38 mm
125 mm
38 mm

19 Fill any small gaps on the bottom surface of the carrier, between the band and the base, with adhesive and wipe off the excess. Sand the bottom surface immediately. This will load the glue-filled crevice with sawdust and ensure that the edge of the band is flush with the base.

STEP 14 Drive copper tacks through the holes in the band using the anvil support and a pipe clamp.

INSTALLING THE BASKET'S CARRIER BASE

20 Drill 2.5 mm holes through the band and 13 mm into the base (see the Full-sized Basket Base Pattern and the Toothpick Hole Detail on the Exploded View diagram, pages 61 and 64).

21 Gently tap a round toothpick through the hole in the band and into the base. Trim the end of the toothpick and sand it flush with the outside surface of the band.

FORMING THE TAPERED HANDLE

22 Cut a piece of 3 mm Victorian ash to 19 x 470 mm long for the handle of the basket (G). Transfer the Full-size Half Handle Pattern (see page 62) and hole locations to both ends of the handle strip.

23 Carefully band saw the four curves to shape. Using the rounded end of a belt sander or a drum sander, give the band-sawed contours a light sand. Drill three 1.5 mm holes through each end of the handle where marked.

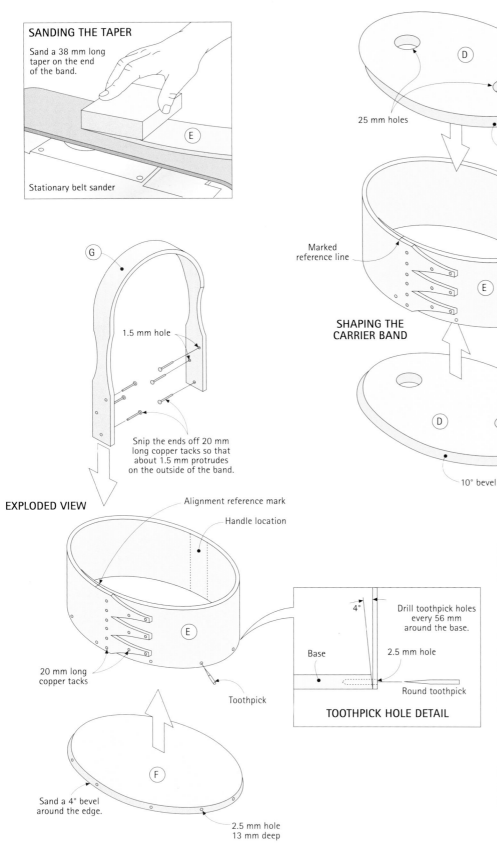

SANDING THE TAPER

Sand a 38 mm long taper on the end of the band.

Stationary belt sander

25 mm holes

D

10° bevel

Marked reference line

E

SHAPING THE CARRIER BAND

D

10° bevel

G

1.5 mm hole

Snip the ends off 20 mm long copper tacks so that about 1.5 mm protrudes on the outside of the band.

EXPLODED VIEW

Alignment reference mark

Handle location

E

20 mm long copper tacks

Toothpick

F

Sand a 4° bevel around the edge.

2.5 mm hole
13 mm deep

4°

Drill toothpick holes every 56 mm around the base.

Base

2.5 mm hole

Round toothpick

TOOTHPICK HOLE DETAIL

24 Follow the same soaking method described in step 10 for the band. Remove the handle from the water and immediately centre and wrap it over one end of the band form.

25 Position the handle in the basket. Apply a small bead of glue to the mating surfaces of the handle and then drive 3 mm long copper tacks from the inside through the handle and band and against the pipe on the support to fasten the handle to the carrier (see the Exploded View diagram, left).

26 For the tacks going through the back of the carrier, drive the tacks through the handle and band, snip 3 mm off the ends, and then drive them against the pipe to clinch the ends.

FINISHING

27 Sand and finish the carrier as desired. The Shakers used milk paints, stains and clear finishes.

Corner Shelves

Brighten up a dull corner with this lovely, country-style shelf unit. The shiplap pine backing makes interesting viewing and gives it a nautical air.

ASSEMBLING THE SHELF

1 Draw a diagonal line across a 320 mm square piece of 16 mm thick MDF. Using a jigsaw, cut along this line to form the top and bottom shelves (A, B) then plane or sand the cut edge smooth. Cut a 50 mm triangular piece from each outside corner (see the Shelf Detail on the Exploded View diagram, page 66). Round-over all the outside edges using a block plane or router fitted with an 8 mm round-over bit.

2 From 16 mm thick MDF, cut a 270 mm square piece for the middle shelf (C). Following the same procedure used for the top and bottom shelves, mark and cut along the diagonal, and round-over the edges of the shelf.

3 Cut two pieces of 60 x 16 mm thick MDF, 630 mm long for the sides (D) and transfer the Side Half-pattern (see page 66) onto each, then flip the pattern over to complete the shape.

4 Cut the curved sides to shape with a jigsaw and sand smooth, rounding the edge slightly (about 3 mm). Install a 12 mm rebate cutter in a router and cut a 8 mm deep rebate in the inside edge of each side piece for the shiplap backing.

5 Mark the position of the rebate in the sides on the bottom shelf and the underside of the top shelf. With the 12 mm rebate cutter, cut another 12 x 8 mm rebate for the shiplap backing. Finish the rebate in line with the side rebate marks.

6 Glue and clamp the top, the sides and the base together. Drive 38 mm panel pins through the top and the base into the sides.

7 Measure the distance between each rebate and cut four pieces of shiplap to length (see the Timber list, page 66). Plane the edge on the first two pieces at an angle to fit into the rebate in the sides.

8 Glue and nail the first two shiplap boards into the rebates on each side, using 25 mm panel pins. On one side, measure the width needed in order for the third shiplap piece to be flush with the inside edge of the rebate.

9 Rip the board to the measured width. Glue and nail the piece in position using PVA adhesive and 25 mm panel pins.

10 Measure the width the last shiplap board needs to be to finish flush with the back of the cabinet. Rip the shiplap board to size and fix it firmly in place using the procedure described above.

11 Mark the position for the centre shelf 315 mm from the base to shelf's centre. Using a square, mark a line across the back of the cabinet.

12 Glue and nail the shelf into position along this line, using 30 mm panel pins.

This triangular unit will look superb filling up empty space in a corner of a room.

TIMBER

PART	FINISHED SIZE IN MM			MATERIAL	QUANTITY
	W	T	L		
A top	320	16	320	MDF	1
B base	320	16	320	MDF	1
C middle shelf	270	16	270	MDF	1
D sides	60	16	630	MDF	2
E frieze	35	16	336	P	1
F shiplap back	150	12	646	P	4
G quad trim	6	6	600	P	1

Material key: P = pine

OTHER MATERIALS

- Woodworking adhesive
- Nails
- Paint or lacquer

TOOLS

- Jigsaw
- Mitre drop saw (optional)
- Plane
- Orbital sander (optional)

Substitute other tools or equipment as desired. Additional common hand tools and clamps may be required.

Always observe the safety precautions in the owner's manual when using a tool or a piece of machinery.

FINISHING

13 Cut a piece of 35 x 16 mm thick pine to 336 mm long. Transfer the Frieze Pattern (right) to the piece and cut out the pattern with a jigsaw. Sand any saw marks with a file, then sand a slight round along the edges. Glue and nail the frieze into position.

14 Fit the 6 mm quad trim around the top of the cabinet, on the underside of the top, mitring at the corners. Glue and nail the quad trim into place.

15 Punch all nails and apply wood filler to the tops of the holes. When the filler has dried, sand and paint or lacquer the shelf with a finish of your choice. The shelf featured here was given an oil-based undercoat, a coat of blue semi-gloss enamel; then it was given a light sanding and a second coat of blue enamel was applied.

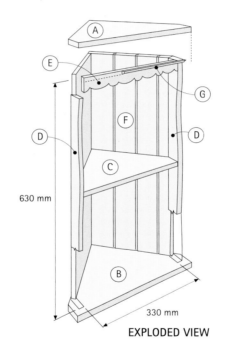

EXPLODED VIEW

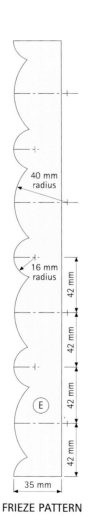

FRIEZE PATTERN

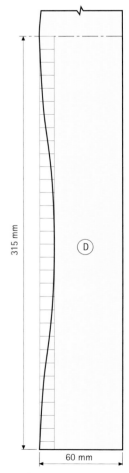

SIDE HALF-PATTERN

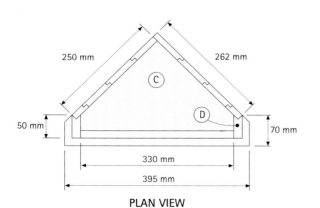

PLAN VIEW

Monk's Seat

Called a monk's seat because of its similarity to a church pew, the lid of this chair lifts up to provide storage for odds and ends. It's assembled from recycled timber pieces.

BUYING AND PREPARING THE TIMBER

The seat featured here is made from recycled oregon, which looks good and is quite inexpensive. The proportions on the diagrams and in the timber list are for dressed timber (recycled timber that has been cleaned up). Page 68 contains a guide to buying undressed timber for the seat at a demolition yard. You can dress this timber down with a planer to make the sizes required, varying the preparation to suit the size. A piece 75 x 25 mm, for instance, can be dressed down to form a piece 70 x 20 mm thick or a piece 65 x 20 mm thick.

1 Pull all the old nails out of the oregon pieces, then clean them up and dress them to the thicknesses in the Timber list (see page 68).

2 Edge-join 480 x 20 mm thick pieces, 1000 mm long, for the sides (A), making sure that they are flat. Remove any excess glue with a wet rag. When the glue has dried, sand the joints flush, using a belt sander. Referring to the Side Pattern diagram (page 69), mark out the shape for the ends. Cut just outside the line with a jigsaw, then sand to the line to form the finished shape.

MAKING THE FRONT AND BACK FRAMES

3 Cut four pieces of 65 x 22 mm thick oregon 600 mm long for the horizontal rails (B) and four pieces 263 mm long for each vertical style (C). Drill a 10 mm hole, 21 mm in from the edge of the stile ends, using a dowelling jig. Make a corresponding pair of holes on the edge at each end of the rails. Insert a dowel in the holes in each stile and rail pair. Glue and clamp the dowel joints, to form the front and back frames, making sure that the frames are square and flat.

4 When the adhesive has dried completely, remove the frames from the clamps and sand all the joints flush. Install a 12 mm rebating bit in the router and cut a 10 mm rebate, 4 mm deep in the inside of the back frame. Cut a 10 mm wide x 8 mm deep rebate on the inside of the front frame. Install a 10 mm cove cutter in the router and rout a decorative mould around the inside edge of each frame face.

5 From 100 x 38 mm thick oregon, cut strips 38 x 4 mm thick, 1000 mm long, for the lattice (L).

6 You can use either a diagonal or a square pattern for the lattice. Place

Combining both storage and seating, this easy-to-build chair takes no time to make.

BUYING GUIDE

PARTS	SIZE IN MM	
	PIECE	TIMBER
Sides, seat	250 x 25 x 4000	RO
Front and back frame, top and bottom back, rail and hinge support	75 x 25 x 6000	RO
Braces, cleats	50 x 25 x 3600	RO
Lining boards	140 x 15 x 2500	RO
Trims	25 x 20 x 1000	RO
Lattice	100 x 38 x 1000	RO
Front, back panels	600 x 3 x 600, 600 x 10 x 600	Ply
Bottom	416 x 10 x 600	Ply

Measurements are linear sizes commonly available for recycled timbers. See the cutting list for a complete set of sizes and lengths.

Material key: RO = recycled oregon, Ply = plywood

TIMBER

PART	FINISHED SIZE IN MM					
	W	T	L	MATERIAL	QUANTITY
A sides*	240	20	1000	RO	4
B frame rail	65	22	600	RO	4
C stile	65	22	263	RO	4
D hinge rail	65	22	600	RO	1
E battens	45	22	445	RO	4
F back rails	70	22	600	RO	2
G cleats	45	22	370	RO	2
H seat*	204	22	596	RO	2
I lining board	140	15	449	RO	5
J brace	45	22	115	RO	8
K base	445	4	600	Ply	1
l lattice	38	4	12 metres	RO	1
M back	283	4	490	Ply	2
N trim	30	10	600	RO	2

* Edge-join to finished width, as stated in the text.

Material key: RO = recycled oregon

OTHER MATERIALS

- **Panel pins:** 10 mm, 16 mm, 20 mm
- **Countersunk wood screws:** 8 g x 20 mm, 8 g x 38 mm, 8 g x 45 mm
- **PVA adhesive**
- **2 x 38 mm decorative brass braces**
- **Finish**

TOOLS

- Jigsaw
- 50 mm drum sander
- Router
- Router cutters: 6 mm cove, 12 mm rebate
- Drill
- Drill bits: 3 mm, 6 mm, 10 mm
- Circular rip saw
- Planer
- 10 mm plug cutter

Substitute other tools or equipment as desired. Additional common hand tools and clamps may be required.

Always observe the safety precautions in the owner's manual when using a tool or a piece of machinery.

to the back of the lattice, then into the back frame rebate.

ASSEMBLING THE CHAIR

8 Cut 22 mm thick recycled oregon 45 x 445 mm long for the bottom fixing battens (E). Screw the fixing battens into the chair sides 30 mm up from the bottom and 22 mm in from the back edge. Screw the top batten 303 mm above the bottom batten.

9 Assemble the frame by counter-boring and screwing through the sides and into the front and back panel. Check for square and twist. Referring to the Step 9 illustration and the Lid Frame diagram (see pages 67 and 69), cut the diagonal braces (J) and fix them to the top and bottom inside corners of the seat frame.

10 From 22 mm thick timber, cut a hinge rail (D) 65 x 600 mm long.

STEP 9 Fix diagonal braces to the inside corners of the seat frame.

the first layer of into the centre of the frame's rebate. Apply a small amount of adhesive to the end of each strip and nail them into position using 10 mm panel pins. Work towards each outer edge of the frame, using a short off-cut as a spacer between each piece. Use the same procedure to place the second row but

position the strips so that they are at right angles to the first set of strips. Cut the ends at the appropriate angle to fit into the frame. This angle will depend upon the slope of the lattice.

7 Using adhesive and 16 mm panel pins, glue and nail the plywood (M)

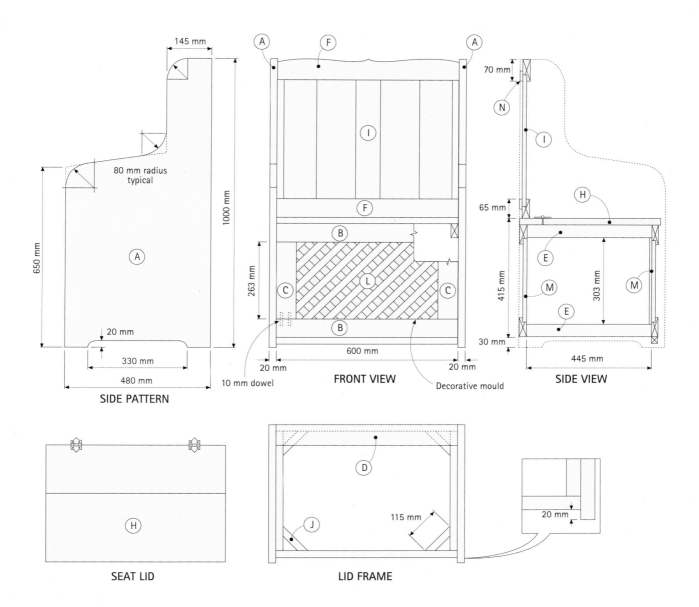

SIDE PATTERN

145 mm

80 mm radius typical

1000 mm

650 mm

480 mm

330 mm

20 mm

A

FRONT VIEW

10 mm dowel

Decorative mould

600 mm

20 mm

20 mm

263 mm

A · F · A

I

F

B

C · L · C

B

SIDE VIEW

70 mm

65 mm

30 mm

415 mm

303 mm

445 mm

N

I

H

E

M

M

E

SEAT LID

H

LID FRAME

D

J

115 mm

20 mm

Glue and screw it into position on top of the back frame, flush with the back of the frame (see the Lid Frame diagram, above).

11 Cut the top and bottom back rails (F) and shape the top rail for the seat back (see the Timber list, page 68). Then, using the router, rebate the back edge of each rail to form a 12 x 12 mm rebate for the chair back lining boards. Counter-bore and screw the top and bottom back rails into position 12 mm in from the back of the chair.

12 Cut the lining boards (I) to length and fix them into the rebate with 18 mm panel pins. Cut two trim pieces (N) 30 x 10 mm thick and fix them into the backs of the rails, using adhesive and

20 mm panel pins (see the Side View diagram, above).

13 Cut the plywood base (K) for the storage box and glue it in position. Edge-join 22 mm oregon to form the seat (H), 408 x 596 mm long. Then, referring to the Step 13 illustration (see right), screw two 45 x 22 mm thick cleats (G) under the seat, 100 mm from each end.

FINISHING

14 Referring to the Seat Lid diagram above, fix the seat onto the hinge rail with a pair of decorative brass hinges. Fill any screw holes with timber plugs and sand the chair, rounding over the edges and sanding the plugs flush.

Then apply two to three coats of clear satin polyurethane.

STEP 13 Screw two cleats underneath the lid, cutting the front ends at an angle so that they fit beside the side braces.

Punched-tin Pie Safe

Before iceboxes became a common household item, frugal homemakers stored breadstuffs in a pie safe. The safe's punched-tin panels weren't just for decoration: the tiny holes allowed air to circulate, preventing goods from moulding but keeping pests away. This pine replica does the same thing, but it can hold a lot more than just pies and pastries.

BUILDING THE FACE FRAME

Unless you already know how to punch tin, follow step instructions 34 to 52 on pages 75 to 76. Or, if you prefer a slightly different look and would like to save a little bit of money, install wooden panels in the side frames, as shown in the photograph on page 73.

1 From 19 mm furniture-grade, kiln-dried pine, cut the two stiles (A) to 76 x 1505 mm long, the top rail (B) to 107 x 355 mm long, and the bottom rail (C) to 44 x 355 mm long.

2 Referring to the Face Frame diagram (see page 74), taper-cut the bottom inside edge of each stile (A).

3 Lightly dry-clamp (but don't glue) the rails between stiles. Referring to the Step 3 illustration below, using a square, carefully mark the positions for each of the dowel holes with a soft pencil (see the Face Frame diagram, page 71). Remove the clamps.

4 Referring to the Step 4 illustration (see page 71), using a dowelling jig

STEP 3 Dry-clamp the frame pieces and use a square to make the dowel-hole alignment marks on both mating pieces.

Punching the safe's tin panels is quite simple and will provide hours of fun.

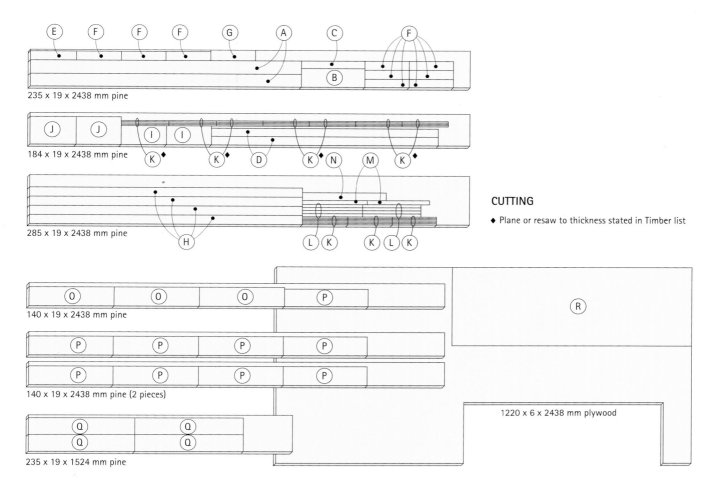

235 x 19 x 2438 mm pine

184 x 19 x 2438 mm pine

285 x 19 x 2438 mm pine

CUTTING

◆ Plane or resaw to thickness stated in Timber list

140 x 19 x 2438 mm pine

140 x 19 x 2438 mm pine (2 pieces)

235 x 19 x 1524 mm pine

1220 x 6 x 2438 mm plywood

for alignment, drill 10 mm holes 27 mm deep at the centrelines. To ensure that all the holes are drilled to the same depth, wrap a piece of masking tape around the drill bit.

5 Glue, dowel, and clamp the rails of the safe between the stiles. Check for square, and make sure that the assembly is lying completely flat. Carefully wipe off any excess glue with a damp cloth.

STEP 4   Using a dowelling jig for proper alignment, drill 10 mm dowel holes 27 mm deep in the face frame pieces where marked.

MAKING THE DOOR AND THE SIDE FRAMES

6 Cut the door stiles (D) and rails (E, F, G) to size (see the Timber list, page 72). (Note: Cut all nine 'F' rails but set six aside for the side frames.)

7 Using the method described above, make the dowel-hole alignment marks, drill the holes, then glue, dowel and clamp the door frame together. Check for square and make sure the assembly clamps flat.

8 Cut the side-frame stiles (H) and rails (I, J) (see the Timber list, page 72). Mark and taper-cut the bottom inside edge of each stile. Make the dowel-hole alignment marks, drill the holes, then glue, dowel, and clamp each side frame. Again, check for square, and make sure the assembly clamps flat.

9 Fit your router with a 6 mm rebating bit. Rout a 6 mm rebate 13 mm deep along the back inside edge of the side frames for the plywood back (R).

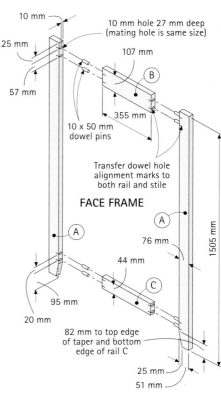

10 mm

25 mm

57 mm

10 mm hole 27 mm deep (mating hole is same size)

107 mm

10 x 50 mm dowel pins

355 mm

Transfer dowel hole alignment marks to both rail and stile

FACE FRAME

1505 mm

76 mm

44 mm

95 mm

20 mm

82 mm to top edge of taper and bottom edge of rail C

25 mm

51 mm

T I M B E R

FINISHED SIZE IN MM

PART	W	T	L	MATERIAL	QUANTITY
FACE FRAME					
A stiles	76	19	1505	P	2
B rail	107	19	355	P	1
C rail	44	19	355	P	1
DOOR, SIDE FRAMES					
D stiles	54	19	1264	P	2
E rail	54	19	241	P	1
F rails	57	19	241	P	9
G rail	73	19	241	P	1
H stiles	57	19	1505	P	4
I rails	121	19	241	P	2
J rails	165	19	241	P	2
K* stops	13	6	254	P	48
CLEATS					
L shelf	19	19	325	P	8
M bottom	19	19	350	P	2
N back	38	19	470	P	1
EDGE-JOINED PARTS					
O* bottom	350	19	470	EJP	1
P* shelves	325	19	470	EJP	3
Q* top	425	19	610	EJP	1
BACK					
R back	495	6	1390	FPL	1
MOULDING, OPTIONAL PANELS					
S sides	51	19	413	PSM	2
T front	51	19	584	PSM	1
U* panels (optional)	254	6	254	EJP	8

Initially cut parts marked with an * oversized, then, trim each to the finished size according to the step-by-step instructions.

Material key: P = pine, EJP = edge-joined pine, FPL = fir plywood, PSM = pine scotia moulding.

O T H E R   M A T E R I A L S

- 10 x 50 mm dowel pins
- 8 g x 32 mm flathead wood screws
- 19 mm brads
- 38 mm brads
- Panel pins: 16 mm, 38 mm
- Stain
- Finish

10 Rout a 6 mm rebate 13 mm deep along the back inside edge of the door-frame openings for the punched-tin panels. Repeat this process along the back inside edge of all the panel openings in the side frames for the punched-tin or wood panels.

11 Use a sharp chisel to square each of the round routed corners in the door and the side frame openings of the safe.

12 Rip and then mitre-cut the stops (K) for all the punched-tin panels. (You could plane 19-mm thick pine to 13 mm thickness, then rip 6 mm wide strips from the edges for the 6 x 13 mm stops.) If you plan to use solid-wood panels, cut stops to 6 mm square and to the same length as those used for the punched-tin panels.

13 Snip the head off a 38 mm brad, and chuck the headless brad into

T O O L S

- Table saw
- Mitre saw
- Portable drill
- Dowelling jig
- Drill bits: 2.5 mm, 3 mm, 10 mm
- Router
- Router bit: 6 mm rebating bit
- Orbital sander

Substitute other tools or equipment as desired. Additional common hand tools and clamps may be required to complete the project.

Always observe the safety precautions in the owner's manual when using a tool or piece of machinery.

your portable drill. Sharpen the point, and use the brad as a bit to drill angled pilot holes through the stops (K) (see the Panel Assembly diagram and the Side View Details, page 73).

ADDING THE CABINET'S TOP, BOTTOM AND SHELVES

14 Cut the shelf cleats (L), bottom cleats (M), and upper back cleat (N) to size (see Timber list, left).

15 Referring to the Exploded View diagram and the Cleat Detail diagram (page 74), drill mounting holes (in both directions), and screw (but don't glue) the cleats to the inside of the side frames.

16 Edge-join enough stock for the bottom (O), shelves (P), and top (Q). Cut the individual pieces oversized so that each edge-joined panel measures an extra 25 mm in length and 13 mm in width. Glue and clamp each panel.

17 Later, remove the clamps, trim the bottom (O) to its finished size and sand it smooth.

18 With the edges of the face frame flush with the outside surface of the sides, glue and nail the face frame to the side frames. Screw the bottom (O) in place to help hold the assembly square while the glue dries. Check for square. Nail the upper back cleat (N) in place.

19 Measure the openings and cut the shelves (P) to finished size. Trim the top (Q) to size. (The top should

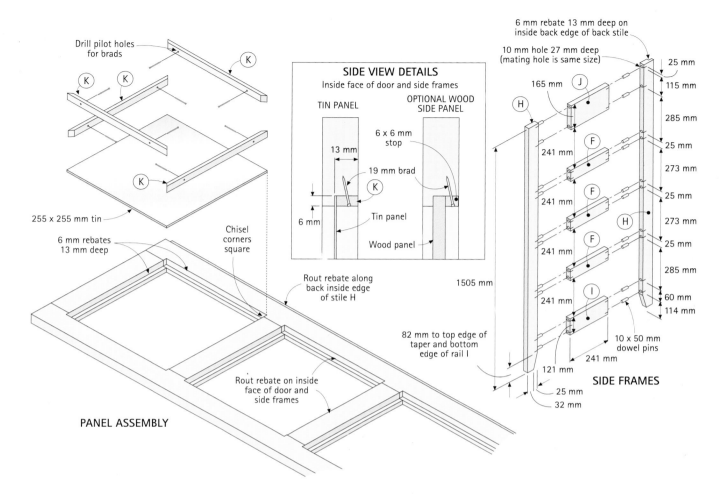

Drill pilot holes for brads

K

255 x 255 mm tin

6 mm rebates 13 mm deep

Chisel corners square

Rout rebate along back inside edge of stile H

Rout rebate on inside face of door and side frames

PANEL ASSEMBLY

SIDE VIEW DETAILS
Inside face of door and side frames

TIN PANEL

OPTIONAL WOOD SIDE PANEL

6 x 6 mm stop

13 mm

19 mm brad

Tin panel

6 mm

Wood panel

6 mm rebate 13 mm deep on inside back edge of back stile

10 mm hole 27 mm deep (mating hole is same size)

165 mm

J

H

25 mm
115 mm
285 mm
25 mm
273 mm
25 mm
273 mm
25 mm
285 mm
60 mm
114 mm

241 mm

F

F

H

F

I

1505 mm

82 mm to top edge of taper and bottom edge of rail I

10 x 50 mm dowel pins

241 mm

121 mm

25 mm
32 mm

SIDE FRAMES

---

overlap the front face frame and side panels by 51 mm.) Sand the parts smooth.

20 Centre the top (Q) from side to side on top of the assembly and align its back edge flush with the back edge of the cabinet. Nail it in place using the 38 mm panel pins. Then, working from the inside of the cabinet, drive screws through the two top cleats (L) into the bottom surface of the top panel (Q).

21 Measure the routed opening at the cabinet's rear, then cut the 6 mm fir plywood back (R) to size.

ADDING THE MOULDING

22 Referring to the Step 22 illustration (right), mitre-cut the side scotia moulding pieces (S) and front scotia moulding piece (T) to the length shown in the Timber list. (Purchase 50 mm pine scotia moulding from a hardware store for these pieces. Then, as shown in the diagram, angle the mitre saw 45

degrees from centre, support the flat areas of the moulding against the mitre saw table and fence, and mitre-cut the pieces to length.)

23 Referring to the Scotia Detail on the Exploded View diagram (see page 74), nail the scotia moulding pieces (S, T) to the cabinet and to the top (Q) of the safe.

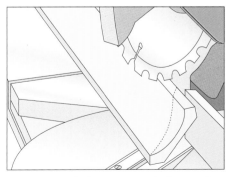

STEP 22 Angle the mitre saw 45 degrees from centre and cut the cove moulding piece, supporting the flat of the moulding against the table and fence.

Wooden panels can be installed in the side frames instead of panels of punched tin, to give the safe a slightly different appearance.

M A T E R I A L S

- 255 mm square tin panels
- Punches
- 1 L distilled white vinegar
- Semi-gloss or satin spray lacquer or polyurethane

O T H E R   M A T E R I A L S

- White cotton gloves
- Pushpins
- Scrap of good quality 19 mm thick plywood, 280 x 280 mm

T O O L S

- 30 mm or wider foam brush
- 500 g hammer

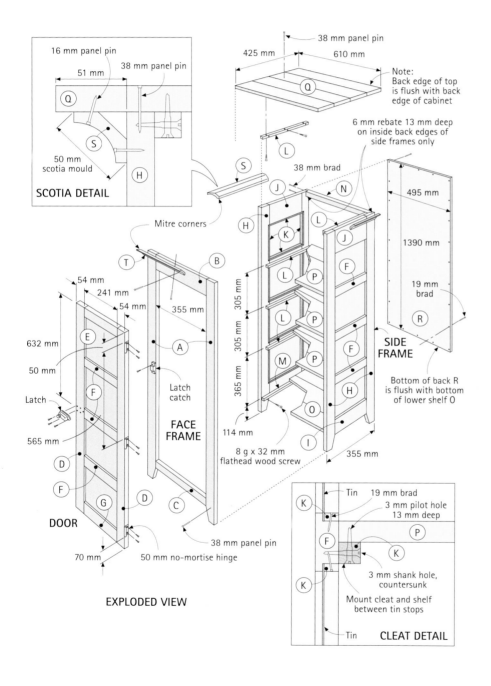

SCOTIA DETAIL

16 mm panel pin
38 mm panel pin
51 mm
50 mm scotia mould

Mitre corners

FACE FRAME

Latch catch

DOOR

54 mm
241 mm
54 mm
355 mm
632 mm
50 mm
Latch
565 mm
70 mm
50 mm no-mortise hinge

EXPLODED VIEW

38 mm panel pin

38 mm panel pin
425 mm
610 mm

Note:
Back edge of top is flush with back edge of cabinet

6 mm rebate 13 mm deep on inside back edges of side frames only

38 mm brad

495 mm
1390 mm
19 mm brad

SIDE FRAME

Bottom of back R is flush with bottom of lower shelf O

305 mm
305 mm
365 mm
114 mm
355 mm

8 g x 32 mm flathead wood screw

CLEAT DETAIL

Tin   19 mm brad
3 mm pilot hole 13 mm deep
3 mm shank hole, countersunk
Mount cleat and shelf between tin stops
Tin

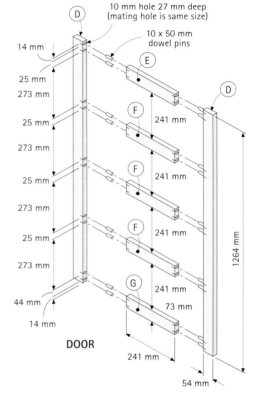

10 mm hole 27 mm deep (mating hole is same size)
10 x 50 mm dowel pins

14 mm
25 mm
273 mm
25 mm
273 mm
25 mm
273 mm
25 mm
273 mm

241 mm
241 mm
241 mm
241 mm
241 mm
73 mm

44 mm
14 mm

1264 mm

DOOR

241 mm
54 mm

FINISHING

24 Finish-sand the pie safe cabinet, door, stops, shelves and, if you are using them, wooden side-panel inserts. Remove the sawdust from the cabinet and the other parts using a vacuum and a tack cloth.

25 Finish the pieces as desired. To give the pie safe a distressed, antique look follow the instructions in steps 26 to 32, below.

DISTRESSING THE SAFE

26 Distress the safe by scratching and denting the parts that would have received the greatest wear over the years. Near the feet, edges and top and around the latch would be the most likely places. Use a ball-peen hammer to make dents, a screwdriver for scratches and a rasp to scuff areas of heavy use. Round-over the edges and corners with 80-grit sandpaper wrapped around a 25 mm dowel (see the Step 26 illustration, below).

27 For a natural 'worn' look, sand the edges unevenly from spot to spot. Take care, however, not to distress the piece too much. Leave those surfaces that would have received little wear over the years untouched.

MAKING THE SAFE LOOK ANTIQUE

28 Referring to the Step 28 illustration (above right), apply a dark stain to areas where dirt would accumulate over time (for example, the base of the legs, around the latch and along the edges). A gel stain is

STEP 26 For an edge-rounding tool, wrap a piece of 80-grit sandpaper around a 25 mm dowel.

STEP 28 Apply a gel stain to areas prone to dirt and grime buildup.

STEP 30 Before the stain dries, lighten any high-wear areas with paint thinner. Don't forget to wear protective gloves.

STEP 31 Using a toothbrush, give the project a uniform coat of fine spattering.

recommended because small amounts are easy to apply. Add the same stain to any scratches and nicks to accentuate these blemishes.

29 Apply a lighter stain to the remaining areas and blend the stains where the two meet. Let both stains sit for a few minutes then wipe away the excess.

30 Lighten heavily worn areas with paint thinner before the stain dries (see the Step 30 illustration, above). The thinner will partially remove the stain, making the area appear worn.

31 Add a bit more character by spattering the surface. To achieve this accent (sometimes called 'fly specks'), first mix two parts gel stain with one part mineral turpentine in a shallow container. Then dab an old toothbrush, or a paintbrush with bristles trimmed to 13 mm long, into the mix (see the Step 31 illustration, below). Practise your spattering technique on a piece of paper before trying it on the pie safe.

32 Place the brush about 150 mm away from the paper, and run your finger through the bristles (see the step 31 illustration, below). Don't overdo it; a little spattering goes a long way. When the stain has dried completely, apply a clear finish.

33 If you are using wood panels for the side frames (U), edge-join enough 6 mm pine to make up eight panels. (To obtain panels with two good faces, plane thicker plywood to a thickness of 6 mm.)

TIN PUNCHING

Punched tin panels lend an authentic appearance and distinctive flair to country-style woodworking projects and will make almost any piece look antique.

Tin panels were not only used in pie safes but lanterns were also fashioned from punched-tin (the panels allowed light to pass while blocking the wind and preventing it from blowing out the candle).

The simple technology and tools for punching tin have hardly changed since the early days. But as you will quickly discover, there are plenty of little tricks you can use to guarantee a high-quality end product.

OBTAINING THE MATERIALS FOR PUNCHING TIN

34 Tin panels can be obtained from a local craft supplier. Each panel should be a thin piece of steel with a plating of 80 per cent lead and 20 per cent tin. Avoid so-called 'black-tin' panels (a heavier-gauge steel sheet without any plating). These panels are harder to punch, rust readily and do not age well. Also steer clear of sheet metals such as galvanized steel and aluminium flashing. These products will not give an authentic punched-tin look.

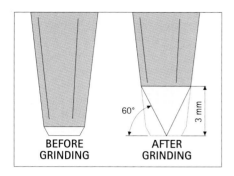

BEFORE GRINDING   **AFTER GRINDING**

35 You can make your own punch for creating round holes by grinding a 1.5 mm nail punch according to the illustration above. With this tool, you can punch a number of different patterns. Some designs, however, require more varied tool tips, such as those mentioned beside the patterns on page 77. (The willow and the star punch are some examples.) Grinding these shapes yourself can be extremely difficult, if not impossible, so you're probably better off obtaining special punches.

36 Some design options for the 254 x 254 mm panels in the pie safe are reproduced on the opposite page. You could also design a pattern of your own and use a photocopier to reproduce it to the correct size.

PREPARING THE TIN PANELS

37 Clean the protective coating away from both sides of the panel using a rag dampened with mineral turpentine or lacquer thinner. Then lightly and evenly scuff both surfaces with 0000 steel wool. Be careful not to press too hard with the steel wool, to avoid putting scratches in the panel.

38 Wash both sides of the panel with dishwashing soap after scuffing to remove the oil residue from the steel wool. Rinse away all traces of the soap with water.

39 You must now be careful not to get any fingerprints, oil or dirty smudges on either side of the panel. These contaminants may cause a splotchy appearance when the panel is put through the ageing process, so every time you handle a panel remember to wear white cotton gloves.

AGEING THE TIN PANELS

40 Spread some newspapers over the surface you are working on and pour some vinegar into a clean, shallow container (a tuna or cat-food tin makes a suitable receptacle). Saturate the foam brush with vinegar and apply the vinegar to the panel in straight, overlapping strokes. Do not retouch the vinegar once you have applied it. Work quickly, pausing no longer than a second or two between strokes, otherwise the vinegar will react unevenly with the metal plating, causing it to streak.

41 Leave the vinegar for five minutes then rinse the panel with running water and dry it with a clean, soft rag. Repeat this procedure on the other side of the panel, being careful not to get any vinegar or contaminants on the side you have just completed.

SECURING THE TIN PANELS

42 Obtain a scrap of plywood that is larger than the panel. (Avoid using low-quality plywood with lots of voids beneath the surface for the base. If you punch into one of these voids, the punch tip will go deeper than intended and create a hole that is too large.).

43 The tin panel will have a slight bow because it has been cut from a large roll. Place the panel, with the peak of its bow up, onto the base. The punching will counteract the panel's bow and may actually cause it to bow the other way.

44 Secure the tin panel to the base with at least six pushpins positioned to hold the panel flat. Centre the pattern on the panel and adhere it with masking tape.

PUNCHING THE PATTERNS

45 Choose a point on the pattern to make the first punch. With the hammer, punch each hole once, keeping track of the holes punched so that none is punched twice. To form large holes strike the punch harder than for small holes.

46 Punch all holes of one size before punching all holes of another size to achieve consistent sizes.

47 Concentrate on cleanly striking the punch so that the hammer does not deflect off the punch. If this happens, you risk striking and injuring your hand or putting an unsightly dent in the tin panel. When the head of the punch starts to mushroom from repeated blows from the hammer, grid it flat to prevent the hammer deflecting. A simple panel pattern can take 20 minutes or more to punch, and your eyes and arms can become tired. To avoid mistakes caused by fatigue, make sure you take good long breaks between punching panels.

INSPECTING THE PATTERNS

48 When you have finished punching, remove all but one of the pieces of masking tape holding the pattern in place. Then carefully lift the pattern up and inspect it to make sure that you have not missed any holes.

FINISHING THE TIN PANELS

49 Before removing the panel from its plywood base, punch a small hole into its corner, no more than 1.5 mm from both of the edges. Remove the pushpins holding the panel in place and pass a length of wire through this hole. Then suspend the panel from the wire and spray both the front and back of the panel with two coats of a clear semi-gloss finish.

50 Punch each of the remaining tin panels, using the procedure described in the steps above. After punching each panel, punch the next panel over an unused portion of the plywood base.

FINISHING THE PUNCHED-TIN PIE SAFE

51 Install the tin panels and then nail each of the stops (K) in place. Install the shelves (P) in the safe and screw them in place.

52 Referring to the Exploded View diagram (see page 74), attach the hinges and fasten the latch to the door of the safe. Then nail the back of the safe (R) securely in place.

TIN PUNCHING PATTERNS

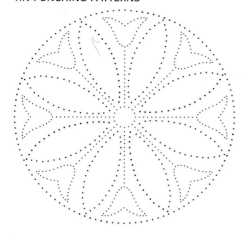

Special tool required: 11 mm chisel

Special tools required:
- Mini chisel
- 8 mm C chisel
- Willow punch

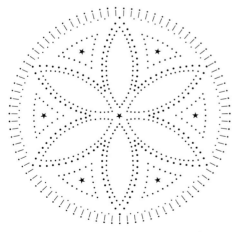

Special tools required:
- 6 mm chisel
- Star punch

All these patterns can be enlarged on a photocopier to suit your panel size. Most patterns can be made using a sharpened nail punch. Others will require special punches. These can be purchased from a craft supplier.

Country Clock

This elegant wall clock combines today's technology with the charm of the past. The simple wooden frame and practical dial recall earlier times; the contemporary quartz movement is easy to install.

Looking for all the world like an antique, this clock is powered by a modern quartz movement.

ASSEMBLING THE CLOCK FRONT

1 Cut two pieces of 165 x 19 mm thick pine 343 mm long. Glue and clamp the pieces edge to edge for the clock front (A). Remove excess glue immediately by wiping with a damp cloth or by scraping lightly with a scraper.

2 When the glue has dried, remove the clamps and trim the clock front (A) to 317 mm square.

3 Draw diagonals on the clock front to find the centre. With a compass, mark a 114 mm radius (228 mm diameter), or a radius that suits your clock face, on the clock front. Drill a blade start hole on the inside of the marked circle and use a jigsaw or scroll saw to cut just on the inside of the marked circle. Referring to the Step 3 illustration (see page 79), tape spacers to the bottom of the clock front to raise it above the drill-press table and drum-sand to the line.

4 Referring to the Exploded View diagram (see page 79), rout a 13 mm round-over along the front edge of the opening. Switch bits and rout a 6 mm rebate 6 mm deep along the back edge of the opening.

5 Rout a 6 mm round-over along the outside edges of the clock front. Keep the bit in your router so that you can use it to rout the frame member later. Sand the clock front smooth.

CONSTRUCTING THE FRAME

6 Cut two pieces of 19 mm-thick pine to 50 mm wide by 762 mm long. Then rout a 6 mm round-over along one edge of each piece.

7 Mitre-cut the frame pieces (B) to 355 mm long. Glue and nail the frame pieces to the clock front (A), making sure that the frame members are flush with the clock front. Sand the frame.

FINISHING

8 Trace the outline of the clock face and the shaft opening onto a piece of 6 mm hardboard or plywood for the dial backing (C).

TIMBER

PART	FINISHED SIZE IN MM			MATERIAL	QUANTITY
	W	T	L		
A front*	165	19	343	P	2
B frame*	50	19	762	P	2
C backing*	250	6	250	H	1

Initially, cut parts marked with an * oversized, then trim them to the finished size according to the step-by-step instructions.

Material key: P = pine, H= hardboard or plywood

OTHER MATERIALS

- Double-sided tape
- 241 diameter dial; high-torque quartz movement with black hands

TOOLS

- Table saw
- Scroll saw
- Drill press
- Drill bit: 10 mm
- Drum sander
- Router
- Router bits: 6 mm rebating, 6 mm round-over, 13 mm round-over
- Hotmelt adhesive gun
- Orbital sander

Substitute other tools or equipment as desired. Additional common hand tools and clamps may be required.

Always observe the safety precautions in the owner's manual when using a tool or a piece of machinery.

9 Drill a 10 mm shaft hole through the centre of the backing and cut and sand the backing to shape.

10 Using double-sided tape or epoxy, adhere the dial to the backing. Check the fit of the dial and backing into the rebate in the clock front. Belt-sand the edges of the dial and backing, if necessary, to make it fit.

11 To 'age' the dial, lightly hand-sand the front of it using 320-grit sandpaper wrapped around a wooden block. Then dampen a cloth with a bit of stain and lightly wipe the front of the dial.

12 Apply a finish of your choice. To reproduce the painted, antique finish used here those parts of the surface that would have received the most wear over the years must be distressed first Follow the technique for distressing furniture described in steps 26 and 27 of the punched-tin pie safe project (see page 75). Then follow the procedure for applying the layers of finishes described in the colonial candle box project (see page 107). Seven coats of finishes, consisting of a walnut stain, a clear lacquer, cajun red paint, soldier blue paint, a mahogany gel stain and satin polyurethane, were applied to the clock in this project.

13 Secure the dial and backing in the rebate with hotmelt adhesive. Drill a hole through the centre to fit the clock shaft. Mount the clock movement to the dial and backing. Referring to the Exploded View diagram (see left), attach the hands to the clock face following the instructions supplied by the manufacturer.

STEP 3 Support the clock front on spacers to drum-sand the opening.

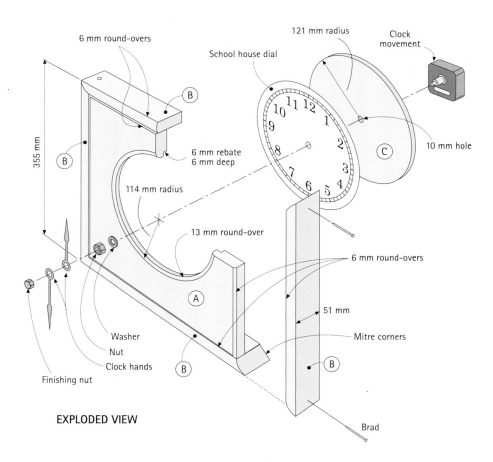

EXPLODED VIEW

Country-style Bathroom

This set of timber accessories will create an appealing country-style bathroom. The fittings are discreet enough to complement a range of decors but will give your bathroom a warm, personal touch.

Country-style bathroom accessories can be difficult to find—now you can make your own.

TIMBER

PART	FINISHED SIZE IN MM			MATERIAL	QUANTITY
	W	T	L		
A sides	150	19	825	P	6
B side battens	50	19	450	P	6
C corner uprights	50	40	825	P	4
D back rail	150	19	1000	P	1
E front rail	100	19	950	P	1
F bottom	990	19	550	Ply	1
G door stop	100	19	650	P	1
H front upright	50	19	745	P	1
I plinth sides	150	19	570	P	2
J plinth front	150	19	1070	P	1
K door	150	19	640	P	6
L door battens	50	19	450	P	4
M top	150	19	100	P	4
N top battens	50	19	500	P	2
O splashback	150	19	1030	P	1
P splashsides	75	19	450	P	2

Material key: P = pine, Ply = plywood

OTHER MATERIALS

- Epoxy resin adhesive; woodworking adhesive
- Wood filler
- Clear satin polyurethane varnish
- 30 and 50 mm counter-sunk screws
- 30mm jolt head nails
- Two magnetic cabinet catches
- Two cabinet knobs
- Four 50 mm brass butt hinges
- 19 x 19 mm scotia moulding, 4500 long
- 10 mm dowel

TOOLS

- Mitre drop saw
- Jigsaw
- Drum sander
- Drill
- Drill bits: 2.5 mm, 4 mm, 10 mm countersink
- Router
- Router bits: 6 mm round-over, 12 mm rebate
- Four 900 mm sash or bar clamps
- Belt sander

Substitute other tools or equipment as desired. Additional common hand tools and clamps may be required.

Always observe the safety precautions in the owner's manual when using a tool or a piece of machinery.

Vanity

1 Cut six pieces of 19 mm pine 150 x 850 mm long for the sides (A). Use waterproof epoxy to glue the two side panels, using three pieces for each. Clamp with sash clamps, making sure the panels remain flat.

2 When the adhesive has dried completely, remove the sides from the clamps. Sand the joints flush with a belt sander. Then trim each of the side panels to 450 x 825 mm long (the finished size).

3 Cut six battens (B) from 50 x 19 mm pine, three for each side panel. Position the first batten flush with the top end, the second batten 75 mm in from bottom end and the third batten in the centre, between first and second battens. Glue and screw the battens to each panel, using 6 g x 30 mm screws.

MAKING THE CORNER UPRIGHTS AND THE RAILS

4 Cut four pieces of 50 x 40 mm pine, 825 mm long for the corner uprights (C). Glue and screw a corner upright on the edge of each side panel, making sure the ends and outside edges are flush with the panel (see the Exploded View diagram, page 82).

5 Install a 12 mm router cutter in the router and cut a 20 x 12 mm rebate 150 mm long in the back corner upright.

6 Cut a piece of 150 x 19 mm pine, 1000 mm long for the back rail (D). Using the router, cut a 20 x 12 mm rebate in each end, to form a tenon.

7 Cut a piece of 100 x 19 mm pine, 950 mm long, for the front rail (E). Mark two holes in each end, 25 mm in from each edge, to form a dowel joint. Mark the corresponding holes in the front corner upright so that the face of the rail is flush with the edge of the panel and so that it is level with the top of the side panel. Using a 10 mm dowel bit, drill each hole 16 mm deep.

FORMING THE BOTTOM AND THE FRONT UPRIGHT

8 Cut a piece of 990 x 12 mm plywood, 550 mm long, for the bottom (F). Using a jigsaw, cut a 20 x 50 mm notch in each corner so that it fits around the corner uprights.

9 Stand the cabinet upright and, using epoxy resin and sash clamps, glue the front rail to the side panels at the dowel joints. Then glue and screw the back rail into the back rebates.

10 Lie the cabinet on its back. Using glue and three 6 g x 30 mm screws on each end, attach the bottom to the lowest side battens.

11 Cut a piece of the 100 x 19 mm pine, 650 mm long for the door stop (G). Fix the stop to the inside of the front rail at the centre, using two 6 g x 30 mm screws.

12 Screw the other end up through the cabinet bottom using another two 6 g x 30 mm screws. Make sure it is square and set 19 mm in from this edge.

This country-style vanity unit can be made quite easily.

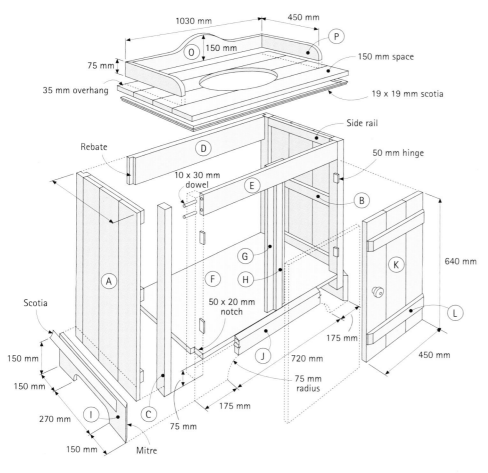

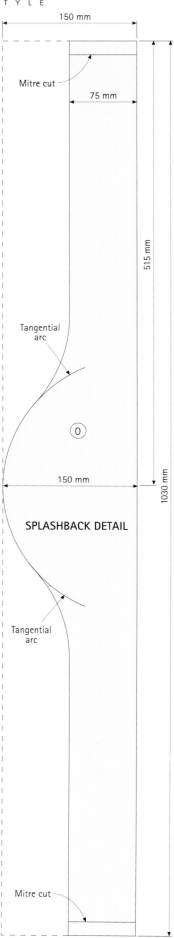

150 mm

Mitre cut

75 mm

515 mm

Tangential arc

O

150 mm

1030 mm

SPLASHBACK DETAIL

Tangential arc

Mitre cut

13 To make the front upright (H), cut a 50 x 19 mm piece of pine 745 mm long. Secure the upright by screwing from inside three 6 g x 30 mm screws through the door stop.

CONSTRUCTING THE PLINTH

14 Mitre-cut the front and side plinth pieces to size (see the Timber list, page 81). On each side plinth measure 150 mm from each end and mark a 75 mm radius (see the Exploded View diagram, page 82). Join the radii up and cut with a jigsaw. Sand the curve using a 50 mm drum sander.

15 Using the technique described above, mark a radius 175 mm from the ends of the front plinth. Cut and sand the curve. Glue and screw the plinth in place, using 6 g x 30 mm screws and screwing each piece from the inside of the vanity, keeping the edges 19 mm below the top of the bottom.

16 Mitre-cut 19 mm scotia to fit on top of the plinth. Glue it onto the plinth then secure it by using 19 mm panel pins.

MAKING THE DOORS

17 Cut six pieces of 150 x 19 mm pine to 640 mm long for the doors (K). Glue and clamp three pieces for each door edge-to-edge. When the glue has dried, sand the joints and smooth with a belt sander. Trim the panels to fit into each door opening, allowing 2 to 3 mm clearance all around.

18 Cut four pieces of 50 x 19 mm pine, 450 mm long, for the door battens (L). Form a mitre cut on each end (see the Exploded View diagram, page 82). Place two battens on each door front, 75 mm in from each end, and insert 6 g x 30 mm screws into the battens from the inside of the door.

19 Hang the doors in the openings, using 50 mm brass butt hinges, and line then up with the battens.

20 Fix magnetic catches to the middle of the door stop and to the backs of the doors. Drill holes for the cabinet knobs where desired and insert.

FORMING THE TOP

21 Cut four pieces of 150 x 19 mm pine, 1100 mm long for the top (M). Glue and clamp the pieces edge-to-edge, using epoxy adhesive. When the adhesive has dried, sand both surfaces smooth and flat. Cut the panel to the finished length (1030 mm), and sand the edges.

22 Mark the cut out for the vanity bowl. Using a 10 mm drill bit, drill a hole as an insertion point and, with a jigsaw, cut out the bowl to shape.

23 Cut two 50 x 19 mm pieces of pine, 500 mm long for the top battens (N). Place a batten across and 40 mm in from each end on the underside of the top. Screw the battens in place.

FORMING SPLASH PIECES

24 To make the splashsides (P), cut two pieces of 75 x 19 mm pine, 430 mm long. Using a jigsaw, cut a 75 mm radius on one end of each piece. Mitre-cut the other end.

25 Cut a piece of 150 x 19 mm pine, 1030 mm long, for the splashback (P). Referring to the Spashback Detail diagram (page 82), mark a line 75 mm from the bottom edge and parallel to it. Draw a curve at the centre of this line (you could use a 4-litre paint can base), then

draw tangential arcs joining the centre arc to the parallel line. Using a jigsaw, cut along the outside edge of the line, then finish-sand to the line with a drum sander. Mitre-cut the ends.

26 Glue and screw through the splashback's mitres into the splashsides' mitres. Install a 6 mm round-over bit into your router and round over the top edges, then sand the unit smooth.

27 Fix the splash unit onto the vanity top by inserting 6 g x 30 mm screws through the bottom and filling the joint with epoxy resin. Make sure that the splash unit is flush with the top edge of the vanity.

FINISHING

28 Remove all the hardware and finish-sand the entire cabinet. Fill any holes with wood filler.

29 Apply two to three coats of water-resistant varnish, following the supplier's instructions.

Wall shelf

1 From 19 mm pine, cut the back (A) to size (see the Timber list, page 84). Referring to the Back Pattern diagram (see page 84), mark the shape for the top edge on the face of the back. Using a jigsaw, cut

Compact enough to position just about anywhere in the bathroom, the shelf is handy for both storing and hanging towels.

TIMBER

PART	FINISHED SIZE IN MM			MATERIAL	QUANTITY
	W	T	L		
A back	225	19	700	P	1
B ends	150	19	185	P	2
C shelf	131	19	700	P	1

Material key: P = pine

OTHER MATERIALS

- 16 x 320 mm length of dowel
- Eleven 6 g x 30 mm screws
- Two 6 g x 45 mm screws
- PVA adhesive
- Paint or lacquer

TOOLS

- Jigsaw
- Drum sander
- Drill
- Drill bits: 2.5 mm, 4 mm, 16 mm Forstner, countersink
- Spoke shave
- Plane
- File

Substitute other tools or equipment as desired. Additional common hand tools and clamps may be required.

Always observe the safety precautions in the owner's manual when using a tool or a piece of machinery.

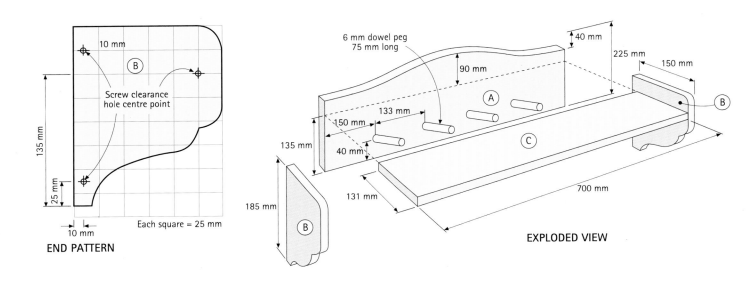

END PATTERN

EXPLODED VIEW

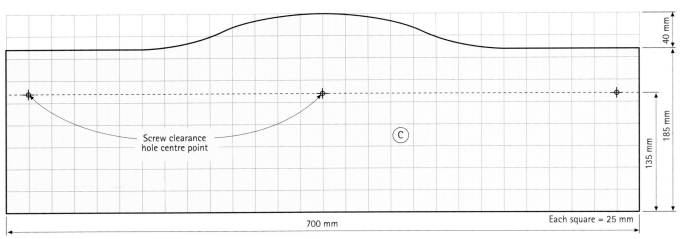

BACK PATTERN

the shape out, working just outside the line. Sand to the line, using a 50 mm drum sander or a spoke shave.

2 Cut a piece of 150 x 19 mm pine, 185 mm long for each end (B). Referring to the End Pattern diagram (page 84), mark the shape of the front and bottom edges on the face of the each end. Cut out the shape and finish-sand it following the procedure used for the shaped back. File the small internal corners smooth.

3 Cut a piece of 125 x 19 mm pine, 700 mm long for the shelf (C). Using a spoke shave or a plane, give the edges of each piece, except those that will be joined, a rustic irregularity, but don't overdo it.

ASSEMBLING THE SHELF

4 With an orbital sander, sand all the surfaces ready for to assembly. On the back, mark a line 135 mm from the bottom edge. Mark three screw holes, two 25 mm from each end and one centred between them. Drill a 4 mm clearance hole and a countersink hole at each mark. Drill the matching 2.5 mm holes in the back edge of the shelf.

5 Apply adhesive to the edge and screw the back and shelf together with 6 g x 30 mm screws, making sure that the ends are flush.

6 Earmark one end for the left-hand side and one for the right, then mark

the screw clearance holes on each (see the End Pattern, page 84). Drill 4 mm clearance holes and countersink holes.

7 Sit the ends into position and use the clearance holes as guides to drill the 2.5 mm pilot holes. Glue and screw the ends onto the back and shelf.

8 Mark the peg holes by drawing a line 40 mm from the bottom edge of the back. Locate the first two peg holes 150 mm from each end and the remaining two holes 133 mm from the first two (see the Exploded View diagram, page 84). Chuck a 16 mm Forstner bit into your drill and drill the four peg holes, allowing the drill to rest against the bottom of the shelf as you drill. This will give the pegs an even upwards tilt.

9 Cut four pegs 75 mm long from 16 mm dowel. Sand one end of each peg round. Apply glue to the hole and insert each peg. Remove any excess glue with a damp rag.

FINISHING

10 Give the whole unit a final sand and apply a finish of your choice, following the manufacturer's instructions. The shelf photographed was given three coats of clear varnish and it was lightly sanded after each coat.

11 Screw the shelf onto the wall by inserting two 6 g x 45 mm screws through the upper back onto wall studs, or by using appropriate wall anchors.

A mirror is an essential bathroom item.

Mirror

1 Cut two pieces of 35 x 19 mm pine, 700 mm long for the sides (A). Mark a 35 mm radius on each end of the side pieces and cut it out with a jigsaw. Smooth the ends with sanding cork and sandpaper.

2 Cut a piece of 120 x 19 mm pine, 325 mm long for the top (B). Scale the Top Pattern (see page 86) to the correct size and transfer the pattern to the top piece.

TIMBER

PART	FINISHED SIZE IN MM			MATERIAL	QUANTITY
	W	T	L		
A sides	35	19	700	P	2
B top	120	19	325	P	1
C bottom	50	19	325	P	1
D back	620	3	345	MDF	1
E mirror	618	4	343	M	1

Material key: P= pine, M= mirror

OTHER MATERIALS

- Eight 8 x 40 mm dowels
- 6 g x 45 mm screws; 13 mm panel pins
- Paint or lacquer
- 620 x 345 mm of cardboard or heavy paper; PVA woodworking adhesive

TOOLS

- Jigsaw
- Portable drill
- 50 mm drum sander
- Drill bit: 8 mm dowel
- Router
- Router bits: 10 mm rebate, 12 mm round-over
- Orbital sander
- Two 500 mm sash clamps

Substitute other tools or equipment as desired. Additional common hand tools and clamps may be required.

Always observe the safety precautions in the owner's manual when using a tool or a piece of machinery.

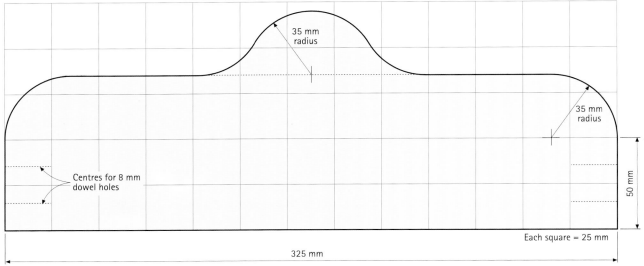

35 mm radius

35 mm radius

Centres for 8 mm dowel holes

50 mm

Each square = 25 mm

325 mm

TOP PATTERN

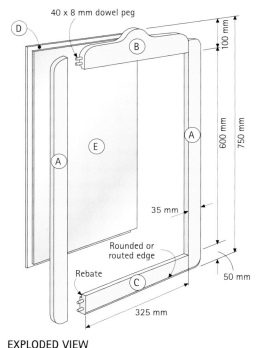

40 x 8 mm dowel peg

100 mm

600 mm

750 mm

35 mm

Rounded or routed edge

Rebate

50 mm

325 mm

EXPLODED VIEW

With a jigsaw, cut the outline just outside the line, then finish-sand to the line, using a 50 mm drum sander or a sanding cork.

3 From 19 mm pine, cut a piece 50 x 325 mm long, for the bottom (C). On each end of the piece, mark the position for the dowel joint by drawing a line in centre and marking the hole positions on this line, 15 mm in from each edge. Drill the dowel holes 21 mm deep using an 8 mm dowel bit.

4 Drill the dowel holes in the top by first marking the centre on each end and then marking one hole 15 mm up from the straight edge and another 20 mm above the first hole (35 mm from the bottom).

5 On each inside edge of the sides, mark and drill matching holes for the dowels: one 15 mm in from each end and another 20 mm from the first.

ASSEMBLING THE MIRROR

6 Using PVA adhesive, glue the dowels into the sides, then glue the top and bottom onto the sides. Clamp the frame joints with sash clamps. Ensure that the frame is flat and check for square by measuring the diagonals. When the glue has dried completely, remove the frame from the sash clamps and sand all the joints flat.

7 Install a 12 mm round-over bit in a router and round the outside edges. Replace the 12 mm bit with a 10 mm rebate bit and cut a 10 x 12 mm rebate around the inside of the frame. Square the corners of the rebate with a chisel.

FINISHING

8 Sand the entire frame by hand or with an orbital sander, slightly rounding over the inside edge of the frame. Then apply a finish of your choice, following the supplier's instructions.

INSTALLING THE MIRROR

9 From 3 mm MDF, cut the back (D) to fit into the rebate (see the Timber list, page 85). Cut a piece of cardboard or heavy paper as packing, to fit between the mirror and the back. The packing will prevent material being removed from the back of the mirror as the back and the mirror move against each other.

10 Lay the frame face on a flat surface and position the mirror (E), packing and back in the rebate. Tap 13 mm panel pins into the inside edge of the frame to hold the back in place.

Toilet paper holder

1 From 19 mm pine, cut a piece 125 x 163 mm long for the shelf (A), and two pieces 112 x 125 mm long for the sides (B).

2 Enlarge the Side Pattern (see page 87), transfer it to each of the sides, and cut them to shape using a jigsaw. Sand the edges smooth, using sandpaper and a sanding cork. (The sharp internal corners may be difficult to sand and you may need to file them smooth.)

3 Drill a hole 10 mm in diameter, 12 mm deep, on the inside of each side, for the paper holder rail. Using an off-cut from a side piece, cut a cleat (C) 32 x

TIMBER

PART	FINISHED SIZE IN MM			MATERIAL	QUANTITY
	W	T	L		
A shelf	125	19	163	P	1
B sides	112	19	125	P	2
C cleat*	32	19	125	P	1

* Cut from the edge of one of the ends.

All the parts can be cut from a single 19 mm thick piece, 150 mm x 450 mm long.

Material key: P = pine

OTHER MATERIALS

- 125 mm long paper holder
- Two 6 g x 38 mm screws
- 30 mm panel pins
- Paint or lacquer

TOOLS

- Portable drill
- Drill bits: 2.5 mm, countersink, 10 mm Forstner
- Jigsaw
- Mitre drop saw (optional)
- Spoke shave or plane (optional)

Substitute other tools or equipment as desired. Additional common hand tools and clamps may be required.

Always observe the safety precautions in the owner's manual when using a tool or a piece of machinery.

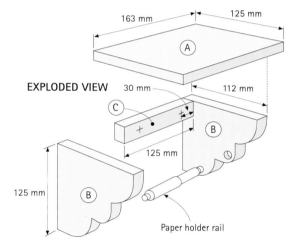

EXPLODED VIEW

163 mm
125 mm
A
30 mm
112 mm
C
125 mm
B
125 mm
B
Paper holder rail

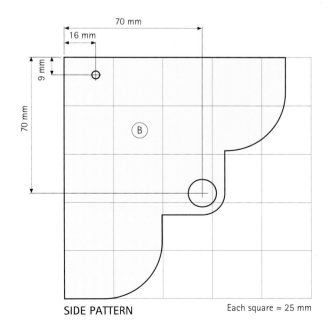

70 mm
16 mm
9 mm
70 mm
B

SIDE PATTERN

Each square = 25 mm

Give every bathroom accessory the country look. The shelf and sides of the paper holder have shaved edges to match the wall shelf.

125 mm long. Drill a 4 mm clearance hole 30 mm in from each end.

4 Sand all the parts smooth. Drill a 4 mm clearance hole 9 mm in and 16 mm down from the back corner of each side, for a 6 g x 38 mm screw, and countersink it.

5 Glue and screw the sides to the cleat, making sure that the holes for the paper holder rail are on the inside and that the cleat is flush with the edges of both of the the side pieces.

6 Apply a bead of glue to the top edges of the sides and cleat. Position the shelf evenly on the sides and fix it in place with 30 mm panel pins. Remove any excess glue with a damp rag.

FINISHING

7 Give the edges an uneven surface, using a plane or a spoke shave (see the photograph, page 87) Then punch all the nails and fill the nail and screw holes with wood filler. When the filler has dried, sand the paper holder smooth and apply a finish of your choice.

Lavatory seat

The seat featured was built to fit a standard size toilet bowl with a width of 360 mm and a length of 500 mm. As toilet bowls vary in size, you will need to determine the size of the bowl of your

A timber lavatory seat adds the country touch where you least expect it.

toilet to calculate the seat and lid sizes required.

1 Measure the width and length of the your toilet bowl and add 30 mm to both dimensions to allow for overhang.

Subtract the width of the seat rail 110 mm) from the length of the bowl to determine the length of the seat (A). (The dimensions of a seat for a standard bowl are 390 x 420 mm long.)

FORMING THE SEAT

2 Draw the seat shape onto a piece of stiff cardboard and cut the shape out as a template. Cut out the central void (hole). The void's shape will be determined by the shape of the bowl, however, it must be parallel to the outside curve and be 75 mm wide.

3 Cut four pieces of 100 x 19 mm pine, 430 mm long. Lie the pieces edge to edge, place the cardboard template over them and trace the shape onto the pieces. Mark the positions for two 8 mm dowels at each join, ensuring that they will not be cut through when the shape is cut out.

4 Using an 8 mm dowel bit, drill each hole 18 mm deep in the centre of the

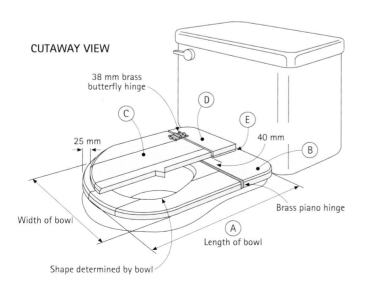

CUTAWAY VIEW

38 mm brass butterfly hinge

25 mm

40 mm

Brass piano hinge

Width of bowl

Length of bowl

Shape determined by bowl

TIMBER

PART	FINISHED SIZE IN MM			MATERIAL	QUANTITY
	W	T	L		
A seat	390	19	420	E-JP	1
B seat rail	110	19	390	P	1
C lid	340	19	435	E-JP	1
D lid rail	70	19	340	P	1
E spacer	70	6	340	P	1

Material key: P = pine, E-JP = edge-joined pine

OTHER MATERIALS

- 8 mm dowel, 1000 mm long
- Two 38 mm brass butterfly hinges
- Twelve 20 x 6 mm rubber screw-in grommets
- One 340 mm brass piano hinge
- Two 60 x 10 mm coach bolts
- 10 mm washer
- Two 10 mm wing nuts
- Epoxy resin; paint or lacquer

TOOLS

- Three 450 mm clamps
- Drill
- Drill bits: 10 mm, 8 mm dowel
- Jigsaw
- Router
- Router bit: 10 mm round-over
- Orbital sander

Substitute other tools or equipment as desired. Additional common hand tools and clamps may be required.

Always observe the safety precautions in the owner's manual when using a tool or a piece of machinery.

end grain. Using epoxy resin, insert the dowels, glue and clamp the pieces together edge to edge. Make sure the boards remain flat when they are clamped. When the adhesive has dried, remove the clamps.

CUTTING OUT THE SEAT

5 Drill a 10 mm hole in the central void so that you can insert a jigsaw blade, then cut out the void, working just inside the pencil line. Cut the outside of the seat to shape, following the waste side of the line. Sand the edges of the outside shape and the void back to the line.

6 Fit a router with a 10 mm round-over bit and round the all the seat's top edges except the back edge. Sand the top and bottom with an orbital sander.

ATTACHING THE SEAT RAIL

7 Cut the seat rail (B) to length (see the Timber list, above). Mark a 20 mm radius on the two back corners of the rail, then cut out the curves with a jigsaw, working just outside the line. Sand the curves smooth to the line. Round over the two ends and the back edge with the router.

8 Hinge the two pieces together using a 340 mm length of piano hinge. Then set the seat assembly onto the bowl

and mark the position of the fixing holes at the rear of the bowl with a pencil.

9 Using a 10 mm bit, drill the fixing holes through the seat rail. Countersink the top of the rail with a chisel, making sure that the holes are deep enough so that the heads of the coach bolts will be below the surface when the seat is assembled.

FORMING THE LID

10 Cut four pieces of 100 x 19 mm pine, 350 mm long for the lid (C). Lie the pieces on a work bench and using the cardboard template trace the outside shape onto the boards with a pencil. Draw an identical shape 25 mm inside the line so that the lid is smaller than the seat.

11 In each joint, mark the positions for four 8 mm dowels. Using an 8 mm dowel bit, drill holes 18 mm deep in the edge of each joint.

12 Glue the lid pieces together with epoxy resin and apply clamps. When the adhesive has dried, remove the clamps.

13 Cut out the lid with a jigsaw and sand the edges smooth. Then round over the curved edge of the lid using a router. Leave the straight section at the back square. Sand all of the faces and edges smooth.

ASSEMBLING THE SEAT PIECES

14 Cut the lid rail (D) to size (see the Timber list, page left). Round the back corners of the lid rail following the procedure described above for the seat rail. Using the jigsaw, cut the rounded corners and sand smooth.

15 Round over the ends and the back edge with the router and sand all surfaces smooth. Attach 38 mm brass butterfly hinges to the lid and rail to hold them together. Cut a piece of 6 mm pine the same shape as the lid rail as a spacer (E). Attach it to the underside of the rail with epoxy resin.

16 Insert coach bolts into the fixing holes. Centre the lid assembly on the seat assembly, setting the back edge of each rail flush.

17 Insert four 6 g x 30 mm screws through the underside of the seat rail to attach the seat rail to the lid rail.

FINISHING

18 Finish-sand all surfaces and apply three coats of a water-resistant varnish, sanding between coats.

INSTALLING THE SEAT

19 Screw 20 x 6 mm thick rubber grommets to the undersurfaces of both the seat and the lid so that the pieces sit squarely on the bowl. Screw four grommets under the seat rail in appropriate positions. Secure the seat under the back of the bowl with wing nuts and washers.

Spice Rack

No kitchen should be without a spice rack, and this model is ideal for using up timber off-cuts such as pieces of maple, skirting and trim that are lying around the workshop. With a little ingenuity it could even be made of gnarled old fence palings.

FORMING THE SIDES

1 Cut two pieces of 90 x 18 mm thick maple, 300 mm long for the sides (A). Referring to the Side Detail on the Exploded View diagram (see page 91), mark the curved shapes on the sides. Scale the Heart Pattern (see page 91) to size and transfer it to the sides. (To add interest, you could invert one heart.)

2 Cut the sides to shape, using a jigsaw or fret saw, working just outside the pencil line so it is visible. Drill a 5 mm hole in the middle of the heart shape so that you can insert a jigsaw or fret saw and cut out the heart shape, again just leaving the pencil line showing.

3 Mount a 38 mm diameter drum sander on a pedestal drill and sand all the curved edges to the lines. Ensure that you do not alter the shape by too much sanding. Parts of the heart will need to be sanded by hand, as the drum sander will not fit inside the shape.

ADDING THE SHELVES AND THE TOP BACK

4 On both of the side pieces, mark the positions of the top shelf (195 mm up from the bottom) and the bottom shelf (50 mm up from the bottom) with a faint pencil line. Cut three pieces of 90 x 18 mm maple, 400 mm long for the shelves (B) and the top back (C). Glue and nail both shelves in position onto each side piece, with the underside of the shelves in line with the pencil line. Remove any excess adhesive with a damp rag. Check that the shelves are flush with the edges of the sides. If they are not, plane or sand them back.

5 Place a 10 mm round-over bit into the router and round over one long edge of the top back piece (C). Sand the edge smooth. Then place the piece on edge flush with the back of top shelf. (The rounded edge should be at the top and the front.) Glue and nail the piece in place.

MAKING THE BACK AND RAILS

6 Cut the plywood back (D) to size (see the Timber list, page 91), making sure that all cuts are square. Glue and nail the back into place using 16 mm panel pins. Remove excess adhesive with a damp rag.

7 Cut a piece of 70 x 10 mm maple, 436 mm long for the bottom rail (E). Using the 10 mm round-over bit, round over one edge with the router, then sand it smooth. Glue and fix the rail into position with 16 mm panel pins, 20 mm up from the bottom edge. (The round-over will again be at the upper front of the rail.) Both ends

This spice rack is easy to make with standard hand tools (plus a fret saw for the curves) and requires no special skills.

TIMBER

PART	FINISHED SIZE IN MM			MATERIAL	QUANTITY
	W	T	L		
A sides	90	18	300	M	2
B shelves	90	18	400	M	2
C top back	90	18	400	M	1
D back	436	3	230	MP	1
E bottom rail	70	10	436	M	1
F top rail	31	10	436	M	1

Material key: M = maple, MP = maple plywood

OTHER MATERIALS

- Woodworking adhesive; finish
- Panel pins: 16 mm, 25 mm

TOOLS

- Jigsaw or fret saw
- 38 mm drum sander (optional)
- Drill
- Tenon saw or mitre drop saw
- Router
- Router bit: 10 mm round-over

Substitute other tools or equipment as desired. Additional common hand tools and clamps may be required.

Always observe the safety precautions in the owner's manual when using a tool or a piece of machinery.

of the rail should be flush with the outside of the spice rack.

8 Cut a piece of 10 mm maple to size for the top rail (F) (see the Timber list, above) and fix it in place using the procedure described above for the bottom rail. (It should be flush with the underside of the top shelf.) (You could use architrave of similar sizes for both the top and bottom rails.) Punch all the nail holes and fill with wood-stopping compound. When the filler has dried, smooth all the filled areas and edges ready for finishing.

FINISHING

9 To give the rack a natural looking finish, first stain the unit a colour you like and then clear-finish it with two coats of polyurethane. For a country-style distressed look like that of the spice rack photographed for this project, finish the rack with milk paint. Mix the paint powder with water and an oil additive carefully following the instructions supplied by the manufacturer. Paint all the surfaces of the rack that will be visible and then dry-finish the paint using beeswax to add depth to the colour.

HEART PATTERN

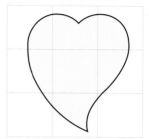

Each square = 20 mm

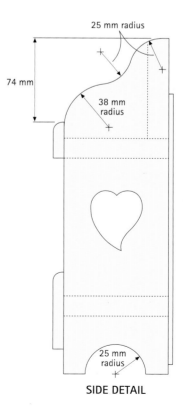

SIDE DETAIL

EXPLODED VIEW

Shaker-style Tall Chest

This simple but elegant cabinet reflects a much simpler time when craftsmanship and practicality reigned supreme. Inspired by a traditional Shaker design, it is loaded with drawers and has a cupboard section on top.

CONSTRUCTING THE FRAME

1 From 19 mm jarrah, rip and crosscut the dresser sides (A), fixed shelves (B, C), divider (D), top (E) and adjustable shelves (F) (see the Timber list, page 93, and the Cutting diagram, page 98).

2 Cut or rout all the rebates and trenches in pieces A, D and E where shown on the Divider and Exploded View diagrams on pages 95 and 96. It is a good idea to apply pieces of masking tape to each piece, marking the good face, top, bottom and back edges This will prevent you from trenching or rebating the wrong face and will prove helpful when assembling the cabinet.

3 Dry-clamp the pieces (except for the adjustable shelves) to check the fit. Set the interior parts (B, C, D, E) 10 mm back from the front edges of the side pieces (A). The back edges of B, C and D should be flush with the shoulder of the rebate along the back edges of parts A and E. Trim if necessary then glue and clamp the pieces, checking to make sure that they are square.

4 Measure the opening and cut the back (G) to size (see the Timber list, page 93, and the Cutting diagram, page 98). Set it aside for now.

ADDING THE FACE FRAME

5 From solid 10 mm jarrah or Tasmanian oak timber, cut the face frame stiles (H) to size (see the Timber list, page 93), but add an extra 1.5 mm to the width. Referring to the Face Frame diagram (see page 95) and the Rebate Detail diagram on the Exploded View diagram (see page 96), cut or rout a 10 mm groove 10 mm deep along the back side of each stile.

Clean lines and a simple, clear finish highlight the natural beauty of the wood.

TIMBER

PART	FINISHED SIZE IN MM			MATERIAL	QUANTITY
	W	T	L		
CHEST					
A sides	549	19	1829	J/TOP	2
B shelves/bottom	534	19	1041	J/TOP	4
C shelves	534	19	518	J/TOP	4
D divider	534	19	1067	J/TOP	1
E top	540	19	1041	J/TOP	1
F shelves	508	19	502	J/TOP	4
G back	1054	6	1753	J/TOP	1
FACE FRAME					
H* stiles	89	19	1829	J/TO	2
I bottom rail	76	19	889	J/TO	1
J top rail	114	19	889	J/TO	1
K mullion	89	19	648	J/TO	1
L rail	19	19	889	J/TO	1
M rails	19	19	889	J/TO	4
N mullions	19	19	137	J/TO	2
O door stops	25	6	502	J/TO	2
DOORS					
P stiles	89	19	641	J/TO	4
Q rails	89	19	244	J/TO	4
R* panels	242	13	487	EJJ/TO	2
SMALL DRAWERS					
S fronts	135	19	432	J/TO	4
T sides	135	13	516	B	8
U backs	121	13	419	B	4
V bottoms	470	6	419	J/TOP	4
LARGE DRAWERS					
W fronts	202	13	886	J/TO	3
X sides	202	13	532	B	6
Y backs	187	13	873	B	3
Z bottoms	470	6	873	J/TOP	3
GUIDES, SLIDES AND TRIM					
AA guides	102	6	534	B	7
BB slides	38	6	464	B	14
CC* bottom front	70	19	1105	J/TO	1
DD* bottom sides	70	19	578	J/TO	2
EE* top front	22	19	1105	J/TO	1
FF* top sides	22	19	578	J/TO	2
GG* shelf fronts	19	19	502	J/TO	4

Initially cut parts marked with an * oversized. Then, trim each to finished size according to the step-by-step instructions.

Material key: J/TOP = jarrah plywood or Tasmanian oak plywood, J/TO = jarrah or Tasmanian oak, EJJ/TO = edge-joined jarrah or Tasmanian oak, B = beech, BP = birch plywood

OTHER MATERIALS

- 10 x 38 mm dowel pins
- 19 mm panel pin nails
- 19 mm brads
- 20 mm flathead nails, 25 mm nails
- Sixteen 6 mm shelf clips
- Clear finish
- Woodworking adhesive; masking tape

TOOLS

- Table saw
- Trench blade or trench set
- Portable drill
- Dowelling jig
- Bits: 6 mm, 10 mm, 11 mm
- Router
- Cutter
- Dovetail jig
- Bits: dovetail, 6 mm round-over, flush-trimming
- Orbital sander

Note: Substitute other tools or equipment as desired. Additional common hand tools and clamps may be required to complete the project.

Always observe the safety precautions outlined in the owner's manual when using a tool or piece of machinery.

6 Cut the bottom rail (I), top rail (J), mullion (K), and middle rail (L) to size (see the Timber list (left) and the Cutting diagram (page 98)).

7 Dry-clamp the face frame together. With a helper, set the cabinet unit on its back. Then position the clamped face frame on the front of the cabinet to check that the tongue on the front edge of the sides (A) fits into the grooves in the back faces of the stiles (H). Then check that the centre rail (L) sits directly over the front edge of the middle shelf (B) and adjust, if necessary.

8 Referring to the Face Frame diagram (see page 95), with the assembly still clamped together, use a square to mark the centrelines for the dowel holes across each joint.

9 Using a dowelling jig for alignment, drill 10 mm holes for the dowel pins to the depths shown on the Face Frame diagram (see page 95).

10 Glue, dowel and clamp the face frame, checking for square. When the adhesive has dried, remove the clamps and excess adhesive. Sand the front and back of the face frame smooth.

11 Glue and clamp the face frame to the cabinet with the ends flush.

12 When the adhesive has dried, remove the clamps. Mount a flush-trim bit in your router and rout the

protruding edges of the stiles flush with the outside faces of the cabinet sides (A) (see the Rebate Detail diagram on the Exploded view diagram, page 96).

13 Referring to the Exploded View diagram (see page 96), cut the remaining rails and mullions (M, N) and, using bar clamps, clamp them to the front of the cabinet.

14 From 19 mm jarrah or Tasmanian oak cut the two door stops (O) to the correct thickness and size. Glue each stop in place behind the top rail (J) so that the stop protrudes 8 mm below the bottom edge of the top rail (see the Exploded View diagram, page 96). This will create a stop for each opening.

CONSTRUCTING THE DOORS

15 Cut the door stiles (P) and rails (Q) to size (see the Timber list on page 93, and the Cutting diagram on page 98). Cut or rout a 6 mm groove 13 mm deep along one edge of each stile and rail (see the Door diagram and Groove detail on page 97).

16 Cut a 6 mm tenon 13 mm long across each end of the rail. In order to do this, mount a dado blade to the table saw and an auxiliary fence to the mitre gauge (crosscut fence). Raise the blade of the saw 6 mm above the surface of the saw table. Then clamp a stop to the mitre gauge (crosscut fence) auxiliary fence.

17 To construct the door panels (R), edge-join timber to form two 254 x 13 x 508 mm pieces. Then trim each panel to finished size, keeping the joint line centred from side to side.

18 Cut 19 mm rebates 6 mm deep along the front edges of each of the panels (see the Door diagram, page 97).

19 Test-fit the door pieces. The panels should be 1.5 mm undersized in width to allow them to expand and contract within the frame. Apply adhesive to the rails and stiles only, then assemble the door parts for each door and clamp. (The panels are designed to float inside the frames of the doors without the use of adhesive.)

TIPS FOR DOVETAILING

• Have the jig at elbow height.

• To prevent mix-ups, number the mating edges of the drawer fronts and sides.

• Adjust the jig and set the depth of the router bit carefully to ensure tight-fitting joints.

• Dovetailed parts should fit together with only a gentle tap with a rubber mallet. If they fit with any play, they will not hold up over time. If they are too tight, you could break them when forcing them together.

• To reduce the chances of grain tearout, make a skimming cut across the inside face of the drawer side by running the router from right to left across the template. Then cut the dovetails to their full depth by moving the router from left to right, following the notches in the template.

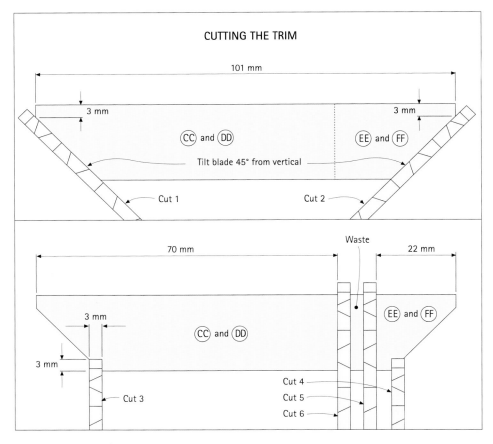

CUTTING THE TRIM

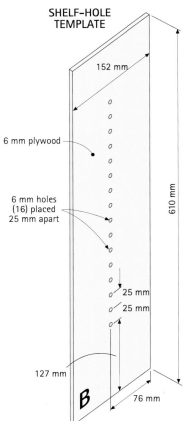

SHELF-HOLE TEMPLATE

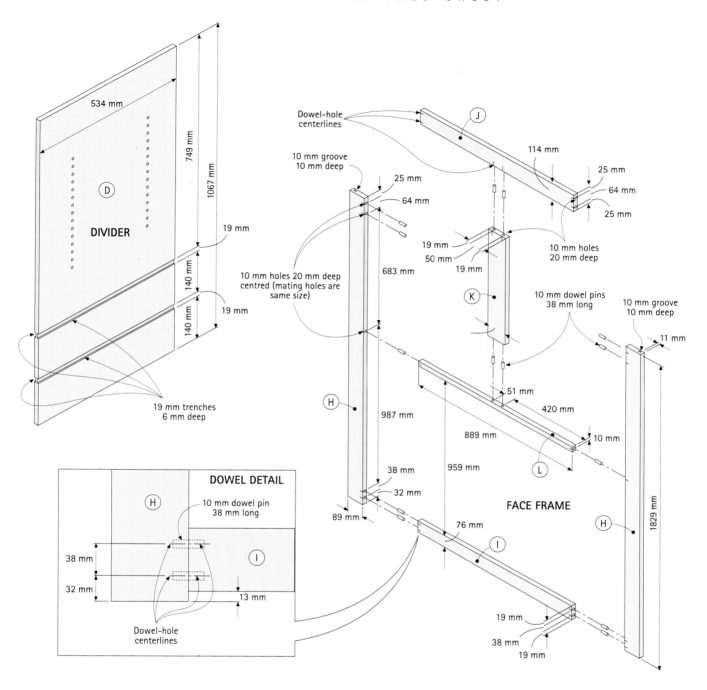

534 mm

749 mm

1067 mm

DIVIDER

D

19 mm

140 mm

19 mm

140 mm

19 mm trenches
6 mm deep

Dowel-hole
centerlines

J

114 mm

25 mm

64 mm

25 mm

10 mm groove
10 mm deep

25 mm

64 mm

19 mm
50 mm

19 mm

10 mm holes
20 mm deep

10 mm holes 20 mm deep
centred (mating holes are
same size)

683 mm

K

10 mm dowel pins
38 mm long

10 mm groove
10 mm deep

11 mm

H

987 mm

51 mm

420 mm

889 mm

959 mm

10 mm

1829 mm

L

38 mm

32 mm

FACE FRAME

89 mm

76 mm

H

I

DOWEL DETAIL

H

10 mm dowel pin
38 mm long

38 mm

32 mm

13 mm

I

Dowel-hole
centerlines

19 mm

38 mm

19 mm

MAKING THE DRAWERS

20 Construct the drawers next, using traditional dovetail joints (see the tips box, right). (If you prefer a simpler method, you could use rebate and lap joints.) First cut the drawer front (S) and back (U) to length (see the Timber list, page 93). Then set the sides and front in the router jig and cut each of the dovetail joints.

21 Set a 6 mm trench blade in the table to cut a 6 mm deep groove 8 mm up from the bottom edge of the

drawer sides and the front. Without changing the height of the trench blade, cut a trench (for the back) into the drawer sides. (You can butt the drawer sides against the fence. You should not attempt this, however, when cutting all the way through narrow pieces.) Cut the rebates on the ends of the drawer back using the wooden auxiliary fence and the 6 mm trench blade.

22 Glue and assemble the drawer, checking for square by measuring across diagonally opposing corners. Make sure that the drawer back does not block the groove that holds the

drawer bottom. Clamp the drawer until the adhesive has dried completely. Then remove the clamps and install the bottom of the drawer, fixing it in place with 20 mm flathead nails. Using a plane and/or a belt sander, adjust the drawer to fit the unit opening. Construct the remaining drawers using the method described above.

ADDING THE GUIDES AND SLIDES

23 Cut the drawer guides (AA) and slides (BB) to size. Sand a slight

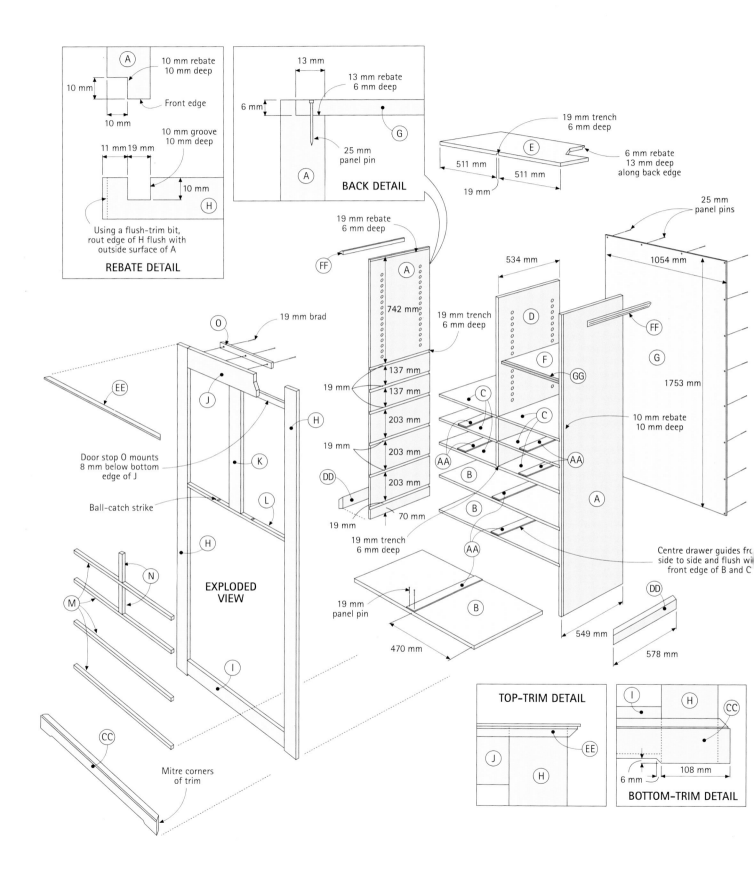

10 mm rebate
10 mm deep

10 mm

Front edge

10 mm

10 mm groove
10 mm deep

11 mm 19 mm

10 mm

Using a flush-trim bit,
rout edge of H flush with
outside surface of A

REBATE DETAIL

13 mm

13 mm rebate
6 mm deep

6 mm

25 mm
panel pin

BACK DETAIL

19 mm trench
6 mm deep

511 mm

6 mm rebate
13 mm deep
along back edge

511 mm

19 mm

25 mm
panel pins

1054 mm

19 mm rebate
6 mm deep

19 mm brad

742 mm

19 mm trench
6 mm deep

534 mm

1753 mm

Door stop O mounts
8 mm below bottom
edge of J

Ball-catch strike

137 mm

137 mm

19 mm

203 mm

10 mm rebate
10 mm deep

19 mm

203 mm

203 mm

**EXPLODED
VIEW**

19 mm

70 mm

19 mm

19 mm trench
6 mm deep

Centre drawer guides fro
side to side and flush w
front edge of B and C

19 mm panel pin

470 mm

549 mm

578 mm

Mitre corners
of trim

TOP-TRIM DETAIL

BOTTOM-TRIM DETAIL

108 mm

6 mm

round-over along the top two edges of each guide. Then glue and nail a guide to each of the fixed shelves (B, C), ensuring that it is accurately centred between the stiles of each drawer opening (see Exploded View diagram, page 96). (When attaching the guides, use a framing square to keep the guides perpendicular to the front edge of the face frame.) Attach duct tape to the front of each drawer to act as temporary handles.

24 Find the centre of each drawer bottom and skew nail the front end of the slides, using two 19 mm brads, to the drawer front (see the Small Drawer Detail diagram, page 99).

25 Slide the drawers into the openings and square the front of each drawer with the face frame. Then, working from the back of the cabinet, mark the locations and then glue and brad-nail the back ends of the slides to the drawer bottoms. (Number each drawer and corresponding opening to custom-fit the drawers to the openings and guides.)

26 Reinsert the drawers and check that the front faces of the drawers are flush with the face frame. Draw a line along the edge of a drawer to indicate where it is not flush. Plane and sand the drawer front even. Recheck against the face frame.

APPLYING THE TRIM

27 Cut one piece of 19 mm jarrah or Tasmanian oak to 102 mm wide by 2400 mm long and follow the six-cut sequence shown in the Cutting the Trim diagram on page 94 to form the trim pieces (CC, DD, EE, FF). Mitre-cut the top and bottom front and side trim pieces to the lengths required by the actual dimensions of the cabinet's sides and front. Then mark and cut the notch along the bottom edge of the bottom front trim piece (CC) (see the Bottom Trim detail on the Exploded View diagram, page 96).

28 Clamp the bottom trim pieces (CC, DD) firmly in place with the mitred ends flush. Glue and clamp the trim pieces to the cabinet and remove the clamps. Attach the top trim pieces (EE, FF).

29 Cut the shelf front trim pieces (GG) to size for each shelf. Glue

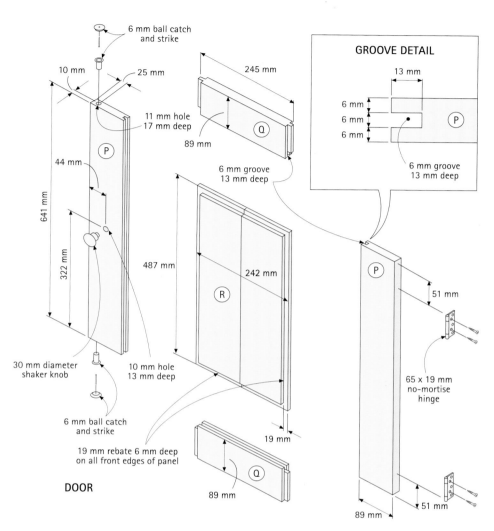

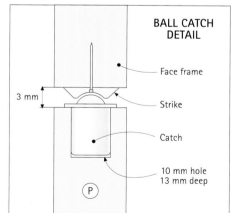

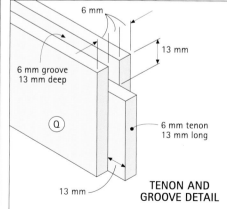

and clamp the trim pieces to the fronts of the shelves (F). When the adhesive has dried, sand the shelves smooth.

ATTACHING THE SHELVES, DOORS, DRAWERS

30 Make a shelf-hole template (see Shelf-hole Template diagram, page 94). Mark the initial 'B' (for bottom end) on the bottom end to prevent you from inadvertently flipping it over.

31 Using the shelf-hole template and a depth-stop on your drill bit, drill 6 mm holes 10 mm deep into the sides (A) and divider (D) (see the Exploded View diagram, page 96).

32 Mark the centre points and drill the holes for the Shaker knobs in the drawers and doors. Mark the centre points and drill the holes for a pair of ball catches in each door (see the Exploded View diagram, page 96, and the Ball Catch detail on the Door diagram, page 97).

33 Add the hinges to the doors (see the Door diagram, page 97). Then, making sure that the gap at the top and bottom is equal, fasten the hinged doors to the cabinet.

FINISHING

34 Remove the hinges from the doors and stiles. Sand the cabinet, the back, the drawers, the doors and the adjustable shelves smooth. Add the finish to all parts, including the Shaker knobs, being careful not to get any finish into the holes for the knobs, the tenons on the end of each knob and in the ball-catch holes.

35 Insert the ball catches and reattach the doors to the cabinet. Mark the mating ball-catch strike locations on the face-frame rails (J, L). With the groove in the ball-catch strike opening towards the front of the cabinet, nail the strikes to the top and bottom rails, centred over or under the protruding ball of each catch when the door is closed.

36 Position the back in the rebated opening, and nail it in place. Glue the shaker knobs in place. Insert the shelf clips into the shelf holes and add the adjustable shelves (F).

CUTTING

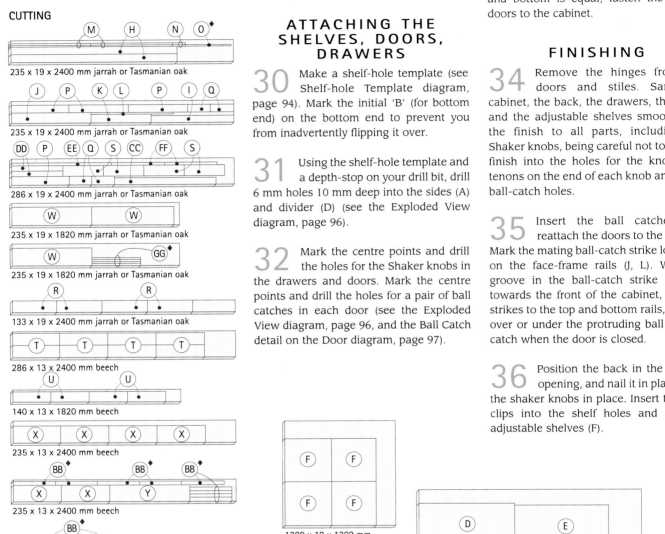

235 x 19 x 2400 mm jarrah or Tasmanian oak

235 x 19 x 2400 mm jarrah or Tasmanian oak

286 x 19 x 2400 mm jarrah or Tasmanian oak

235 x 19 x 1820 mm jarrah or Tasmanian oak

235 x 19 x 1820 mm jarrah or Tasmanian oak

133 x 19 x 2400 mm jarrah or Tasmanian oak

286 x 13 x 2400 mm beech

140 x 13 x 1820 mm beech

235 x 13 x 2400 mm beech

235 x 13 x 2400 mm beech

235 x 13 x 1820 mm beech

235 x 13 x 2400 mm beech

1200 x 19 x 2400 mm jarrah or Tasmanian oak plywood

1200 x 19 x 1200 mm jarrah or Tasmanian oak plywood

1200 x 19 x 2400 mm jarrah or Tasmanian oak plywood

1200 x 19 x 2400 mm jarrah or Tasmanian oak plywood

1200 x 19 x 2400 mm jarrah or Tasmanian oak plywood

1200 x 19 x 2400 mm jarrah or Tasmanian oak plywood

♦ Plane or resaw to thickness stated in Timber list

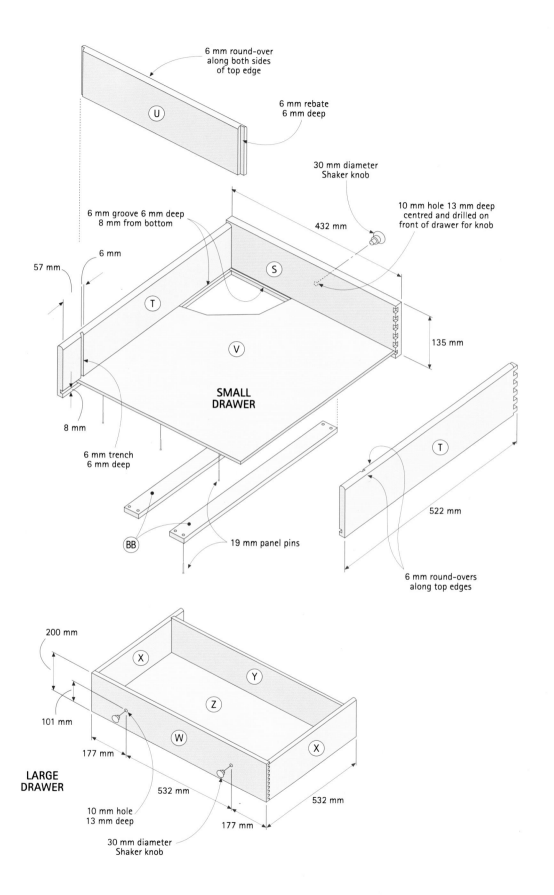

6 mm round-over
along both sides
of top edge

U

6 mm rebate
6 mm deep

30 mm diameter
Shaker knob

10 mm hole 13 mm deep
centred and drilled on
front of drawer for knob

6 mm groove 6 mm deep
8 mm from bottom

432 mm

6 mm

57 mm

S

T

135 mm

V

SMALL
DRAWER

8 mm

6 mm trench
6 mm deep

BB

19 mm panel pins

T

522 mm

6 mm round-overs
along top edges

200 mm

X

Y

Z

101 mm

W

X

177 mm

LARGE
DRAWER

532 mm

10 mm hole
13 mm deep

532 mm

30 mm diameter
Shaker knob

177 mm

Oak Breakfast Tray

This classic tray can be used to serve just about any refreshment, from desserts in front of the television to appetisers at a party or drinks on the patio. Box joints and durable oak combine to make it as tough as it is attractive.

For this project, 13 mm oak is required. To obtain oak this thickness, resaw thicker timber or order 13 mm oak from your local timber yard.

BUILDING THE JIG

1 Referring to the Box-Joint Jig diagram (see page 101), build a box-joint jig by first cutting plywood to size for the fence of your table saw, then pine for the stop block. Glue and clamp the two pine pieces to make the stop block.

2 Unplug the table saw. Remove the table insert and trace its outline on a piece of 6 mm hardboard. (Plane the hardboard to a greater thickness if the table saw requires it.) The top of the insert should sit flush with the surface of the saw table. Cut and sand the edges until the insert fits snugly in the recess.

3 Mount a dado blade or dado-blade set to your table saw and set it to cut 6 mm wide. Lower the saw blade down so that the blade will be below the table insert. Position the insert in the saw-table recess and clamp a piece of scrap timber 100 x 50 mm across (but not directly over) the centre of the insert. Plug the saw in and start the motor. Raise the rotating blade so that it cuts through the insert to a cutting height of 16 mm. Turn the saw off and lower the blade back to a cutting height of 10 mm. Remove the scrap timber.

4 Clamp the jig fence securely to the mitre gauge (cross-cut fence) and square the mitre gauge and jig fence with the dado blade. Run the jig fence across the dado blade to cut the first kerf.

5 Remove the jig fence from the mitre gauge, measure across exactly 6 mm and mark the position of the second kerf (see the Box-Joint Jig diagram, page 101). (If your dado blade cuts a fraction narrower or wider than 6 mm, adjust the size of the gap accordingly.)

Elevated handles make the tray easy to hold and carry.

6 Refasten the jig fence to the mitre gauge. Raise the blade to 13 mm above the surface of the saw table and cut the second kerf exactly where marked. Cut the guide pin to size (see Box-Joint diagram, page 101) and glue it in the first kerf. Remove any excess adhesive.

CUTTING THE BOX JOINTS

7 From 13 mm oak, rip and cross-cut the two tray sides (A) to 610 x 54 mm and the two tray ends (B) to 305 x 97 mm. (The extra width allows for final trimming later.)

8 Referring to Step 1 of the Starting with a Notch diagram (see page 102), cut the first notch. (It is a good idea to test-cut box joints in scrap material the same thickness as the tray sides and ends before you cut the ends of the tray sides and

ends.) Use a stop block to ensure that the edge of the side remains square with the saw table when you make the first cut. Clamp one of the tray sides (A) to the box-joint jig with the left edge of the tray side perfectly in line with the left edge of the kerf. Clamp the stop in position and clamp the tray side to the jig, making sure it sits flush on the saw table, not the insert, to ensure that all the notches will be the same depth.

9 Reposition the tray side and the stop block so that the notch rests on the guide pin and make the second cut (see Step 2 of the diagram, page 102). Referring to the Step 9 illustration (see page 101), make the rest of the cuts, repositioning the tray side and the stop block for each cut.

10 Flip the tray side end over end and cut the notches. Keep the edge that will eventually be the bottom

TIMBER

PART	FINISHED SIZE IN MM			MATERIAL	QUANTITY
	W	T	L		
A* sides	44	13	610	O	2
B* ends	89	13	305	O	2
C bottom panel	299	6	604	O ply	1
D* panel stops	10	6	299	O	2
E* panel stops	10	6	604	O	2

Initially cut parts marked with an * oversized, then trimmed them to the finished size according to the step-by-step instructions.

Material key: O = oak, O ply = oak ply

OTHER MATERIALS

- Stain
- Polyurethane
- 0000 steel wool
- Double-faced tape
- Paste wax

edge of the tray against the stop block when cutting the opposite end so that you form a notch on the bottom edge of each end (see Step 2 of the diagram, page 102). Cut the box joints on the ends of the second tray side.

11 Referring to Step 1 of the Starting with a Finger diagram (page 102), make the first finger. You will need to position the tray end tightly against the guide pin and clamp the stop block firmly in position.

12 Referring to Step 2 of the diagram (page 102), reposition the tray end

and the stop block so that the notch sits on the guide pin and make the second cut. Form the remaining fingers, repositioning the tray end for each cut, then flip the piece end over end and cut the fingers on the other end, keeping the bottom edge of the tray end against the stop block. Cut the fingers on both ends of the other end piece.

ATTACHING THE ENDS

13 Using double-sided tape, attach the two end pieces (B), keeping the bottom and side edges flush. Referring to the End View diagram (page 102), mark the handle shape and opening on one.

14 Using a band saw or a jigsaw, cut slightly outside the marked outline of the handle.

15 Mount a 63 mm sanding drum in a drill press. Referring to the Step 15 illustration (below), attach a fence and a stop block to the drill-press table to help keep sanding uniform, then sand the concave edges of the handle smooth, being careful not to burn the wood. (You could also use the front roller on a belt sander.)

16 Using a drill press with a 25 mm Forstner bit, drill a hole at each end of the handle slot, backing the handle with scrap to prevent chip-out. Remove the timber left between the two holes with a jigsaw or scroll saw. Sand the inside edges of the slots smooth.

17 Separate the two ends and scrape off any tape residue. Using a 3 mm round-over bit, rout both inside edges of the handle slots. (If you don't have this bit, hand-sand a slight round-over.)

STEP 9   Reposition the tray side and the stop block for each cut to form the row of notches in the edge of the tray side piece.

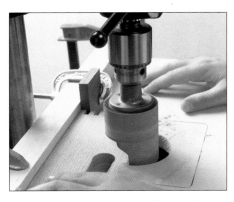

STEP 15   Attach a fence and a stop block to the drill-press table to ensure that the concave edges are sanded evenly.

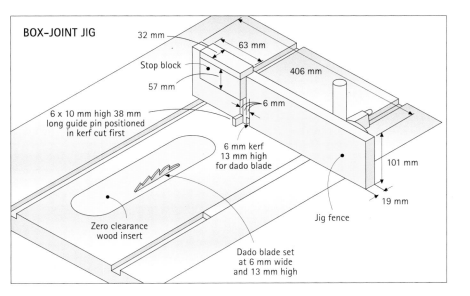

BOX-JOINT JIG

32 mm

63 mm

Stop block

57 mm

406 mm

6 mm

6 x 10 mm high 38 mm long guide pin positioned in kerf cut first

6 mm kerf 13 mm high for dado blade

101 mm

19 mm

Jig fence

Zero clearance wood insert

Dado blade set at 6 mm wide and 13 mm high

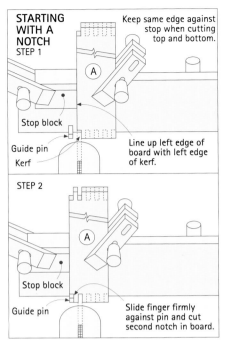

STARTING WITH A NOTCH
STEP 1

Keep same edge against stop when cutting top and bottom.

A

Stop block

Guide pin

Kerf

Line up left edge of board with left edge of kerf.

STEP 2

A

Stop block

Guide pin

Slide finger firmly against pin and cut second notch in board.

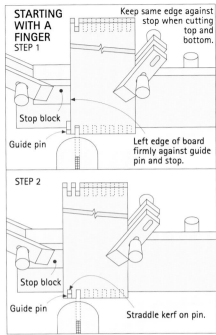

STARTING WITH A FINGER
STEP 1

Keep same edge against stop when cutting top and bottom.

Stop block

Guide pin

Left edge of board firmly against guide pin and stop.

STEP 2

Stop block

Guide pin

Straddle kerf on pin.

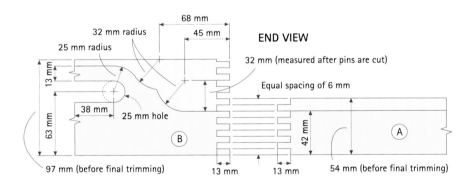

END VIEW

68 mm

45 mm

32 mm radius

25 mm radius

13 mm

63 mm

38 mm

25 mm hole

97 mm (before final trimming)

32 mm (measured after pins are cut)

Equal spacing of 6 mm

42 mm

A

B

13 mm

13 mm

54 mm (before final trimming)

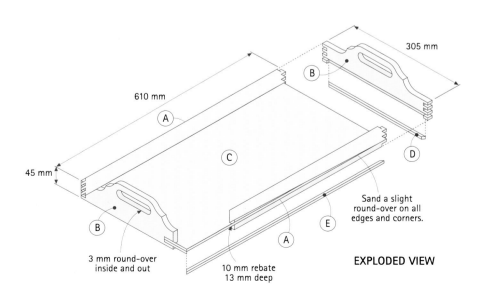

610 mm

305 mm

A

B

B

C

D

45 mm

Sand a slight round-over on all edges and corners.

E

A

3 mm round-over inside and out

10 mm rebate 13 mm deep

EXPLODED VIEW

ASSEMBLING THE TRAY

18 Dry-fit the ends and sides together and mark the finished width on the top edge of the sides against the finished shape of the ends. Disassemble the pieces then rip the sides to width according to your marks. Sand the parts smooth.

19 Glue and clamp the sides and ends together, checking for square. (Use a small brush to 'paint' the glue into the notches.)

20 Remove glue squeeze-out from the inside of the corners with a damp rag. To ensure that the tray will sit flat, place waxed paper under the glued box joints, and clamp the tray frame to a flat surface, such as the saw table.

21 Rout a 10 mm rebate 13 mm deep along the inside of the bottom edge of the tray using a router with a 10 mm rebating bit. (Make two passes using a table-mounted router, raising the bit for the second pass to achieve the depth needed.) Use a sharp chisel to square out the rebates in each of the four corners.

22 Cut the bottom panel (C) to size from 6 mm oak plywood. Check the fit of the panel in the rebate in the tray frame and trim if necessary.

23 From 19 mm oak, rip enough 10 x 6 mm strips for the bottom panel stops (D, E) (see the Timber list, page 101). Mitre-cut the panel stops to finished length. With the bottom panel in place, glue and clamp the stops in place. Wipe off glue squeeze-out with a damp rag.

FINISHING

24 When the glue has dried, finish-sand the tray. Be careful when sanding the box-jointed corners not to burn the exposed end grain. Hand-sand the handle opening until it is smooth to the touch. Then sand a very slight round-over on all edges of the handle to break the sharp edges.

25 Apply a stain to the tray. Follow this with two coats of polyurethane. To give the tray extra protection and to provide a smooth finish, apply paste wax.

Colonial Wall Box

This simple wall box has its roots firmly in the past. In colonial times, similar boxes held long-stemmed clay pipes. These days, wall boxes are ideal for storing matches by a fireplace.

CUTTING THE PARTS

1 Resaw a piece of 19 mm pine to a thickness of 6 mm, then cut the piece 57 x 350 mm long for the box back (A). Enlarge the Top Pattern outline (below) 117 per cent and transfer it and hole centre point to one end of the pine. Drill the 6 mm hole and cut the back to shape.

2 Cut the sides (B), front (C) and bottom (D) to size (see the Timber list (page 104) and the Exploded View Diagram (page 104).

CARVING THE HEART

3 Referring to the Exploded View diagram (see page 104), using carbon paper, transfer the Full-sized Heart Pattern (see page 106) to the front (C).

4 Carve the outline of the heart 3 mm deep with a wood-carving chisel or a craft knife. Then, using a 6 mm chisel,

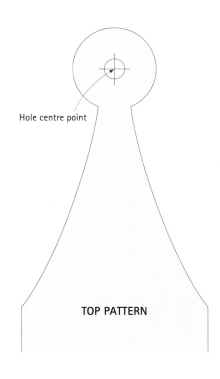

Hole centre point

TOP PATTERN

The box's antique, painted finish gives it an old-world charm.

TIMBER

| | FINISHED SIZE IN MM | | | | |
PART	W	T	L	MATERIAL	QUANTITY
A back	57	6	350	P	1
B sides	25	6	241	P	2
C front	57	6	241	P	1
D bottom	57	6	37	P	1

Material key: P = pine

OTHER MATERIALS

- Double-sided tape; carbon paper
- 13 mm brads
- Woodworking adhesive; finish

TOOLS

- Table saw
- Band saw or scroll saw
- Wood-carving chisel or craft knife
- Drill
- Drill bit: 6 mm
- Orbital sander

Substitute other tools and equipment as desired. Additional common hand tools and clamps may be required.

Always observe the safety precautions in the owner's manual when using a tool or a piece of machinery

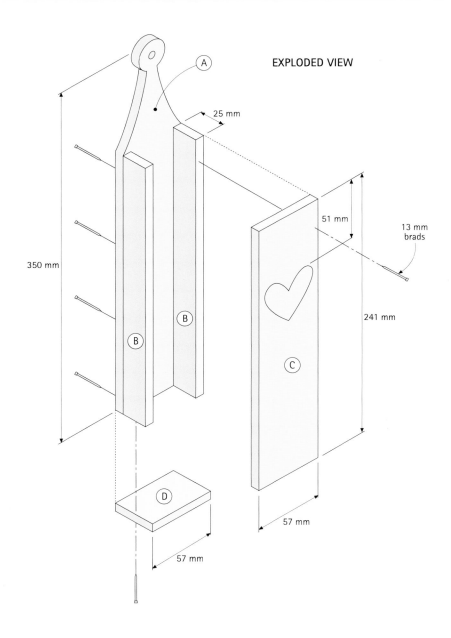

EXPLODED VIEW

remove the timber inside the cut outline. (To prevent the lid moving when you carve, secure it to the workbench top with double-faced tape.)

5 Apply glue to the mating surfaces and hold the box together with tape. Nail the box together with 13 mm brads. Using a nail punch, indent the nails slightly below the wood's surface.

FINISHING

6 Sand and paint the wall box. To reproduce the antique painted look of the box photographed, first distress those parts of the surface that would have received the most wear over the years. On the front of the box, and around the edges of the top and the bottom would be the most likely places. Use a ball-peen hammer to make dents, a screwdriver to scratch the box and a rasp to scuff areas of heavy use. Round-over the edges and the corners with 80-grit sandpaper wrapped around a 25 mm dowel (see the step illustrations in the punched-tin pie safe project, page 75). For a natural 'worn' look, sand the edges unevenly from spot to spot. Take care, however, not to distress the piece too much. Leave those surfaces that would have received little wear over the years untouched.

7 Next follow the procedure for applying the layers of finishes described in the candle box project (see page 107). Seven coats of finishes, consisting of a walnut stain, a clear lacquer, cajun red paint, soldier blue paint, a mahogany gel stain and satin polyurethane, were applied to the clock in this project.

Colonial Candle Box

Early woodworkers built candle boxes to store the valuable commodity. The boxes protected the candles from heat and from mice, which feasted on the tallow shafts. Like many of the originals, the lid on this pine box contains a simple-to-carve decorative motif and thumb grasp.

CUTTING THE BOX PARTS

1 Cut a piece of 89 x 13 mm thick pine, 610 mm long for the box sides (A) and back (B), and a piece of 76 x 13 mm thick pine, 101 mm long for the front (C).

2 Cut 6 mm grooves 6 mm deep, 6 mm from the top and bottom edges of the 610 mm long piece (see the Exploded View diagram, page 107).

3 Cut the same-sized groove as above 6 mm from the bottom edge of the front piece. (Use a 6 mm dado blade to make the cuts or fit your table-mounted router with a 6 mm straight bit and fence.)

4 Cross-cut the sides (A) and back (B) to length from the 610 mm-long grooved board (see the Timber list, page 106).

5 Cut the box bottom (D) to size from 6 mm plywood. Make sure that the bottom is 1.5 mm smaller in length and width than the opening to allow for expansion and contraction of the box. Dry-clamp the box together to check the fit.

ASSEMBLING THE BOX AND PLUGGING THE GROOVES

6 Glue and clamp the box but do not glue the bottom in place as it will float in the grooves.

7 Nail the box together with 25 mm brads. Check for square. Using a nail punch, indent the nails slightly below the surface. With a dovetail saw, cut a 6 x 6 mm thick piece of pine, 305 mm long. Crosscut six pieces 10 mm long from this for the groove filler blocks.

The box's lid slides neatly open and shut, making its contents accessible and keeping it secure.

TIMBER

PART	FINISHED SIZE IN MM			MATERIAL	QUANTITY
	W	T	L		
A* sides	89	13	222	P	2
B* back	89	13	101	P	1
C front	76	13	101	P	1
D bottom	112	6	208	Ply	1
E lid	112	13	216	P	1

Initially cut parts marked with an * oversized, then trim them to the finished size according to the step-by-step instructions.

Material key: P = pine, Ply = plywood

OTHER MATERIALS

- Carbon paper
- Double-sided tape
- Woodworking adhesive
- 25 x 17 mm brads
- Finish: Walnut stain, satin polyurethane, cajun red paint, soldier blue paint, mahogany gel stain, mineral turpentine
- 320-grit paper

TOOLS

- Table saw
- Dado blade or dado set
- Craft knife
- 6 mm chisel

Substitute other tools and equipment as desired. Additional common hand tools and clamps may be required.

Always observe the safety precautions in the owner's manual when using a tool or a piece of machinery.

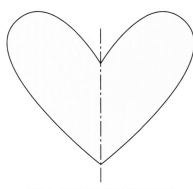

FULL-SIZE HEART PATTERN

8 Glue the filler blocks in the ends of the exposed grooves. When the adhesive has dried completely, trim and sand the ends of the blocks flush with the surfaces of the box.

CUTTING AND SHAPING THE LID

9 Cut the lid (E) to size. (see the Timber list, above). Using carbon paper, transfer the Full-size Heart Pattern (see right) to the top of the lid.

10 With a wood-carving chisel or a craft knife, carve the outline of the heart approximately 3 mm deep. Then use a 6 mm chisel or a carving gouge to remove the timber inside the carved outline of the heart. (To prevent the lid moving about while you carve, secure it to workbench top with double-sided tape.) For a rustic look, leave the faceted chisel cuts visible.

11 Transfer the Full-size Thumb-grasp Pattern (see page 107) onto the lid using carbon paper.

12 Referring to the Thumb-grasp Detail diagram (see page 107), cut the thumb grasp. Using a craft knife or a wood-carving chisel, make a 3 mm deep cut along the straight line. Then, working from the centreline, make an angled cut back to the straight cut, twisting the knife in an arch back to the outer end of the straight line. Repeat this procedure for the other side.

13 Referring to the Cutting Bevels diagram (see left), cut a bevel along three sides of the lid. To do this, tilt the blade of the saw to 15 degrees, then raise it 19 mm above the bench. Set a fence 6 mm away from the blade. Place one side of the lid (E) against the saw fence and make the 15-degree cut.

14 Next cut the other side of the lid and across one end, leaving a 6 mm edge along three sides. Switch to a 6 mm dado blade and cut a rebate along the same three sides of the lid (see Cutting the Rebates diagram, left).

15 Check the fit of the lid in the grooves in the box and trim it, if necessary, so that the lid of the box will slide closed smoothly.

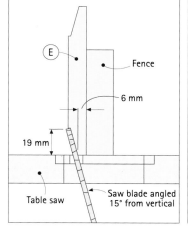

CUTTING BEVELS

E
Fence
6 mm
19 mm
Table saw
Saw blade angled 15° from vertical

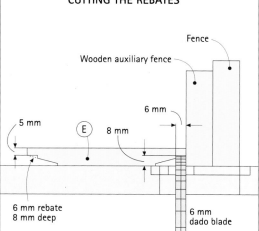

CUTTING THE REBATES

Fence
Wooden auxiliary fence
6 mm
5 mm
E
8 mm
6 mm rebate 8 mm deep
6 mm dado blade

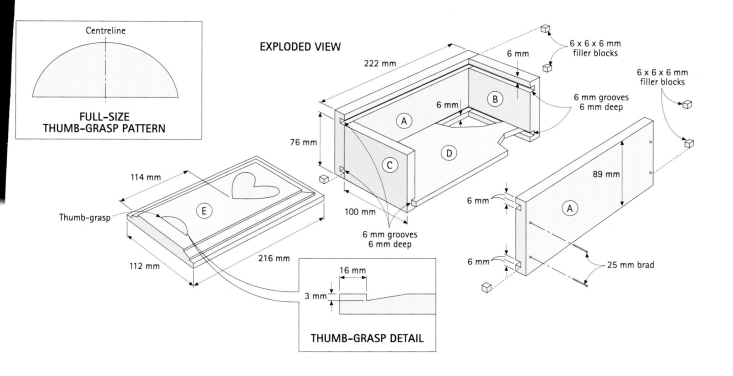

FULL–SIZE
THUMB–GRASP PATTERN

Centreline

EXPLODED VIEW

222 mm

6 mm

6 x 6 x 6 mm
filler blocks

6 x 6 x 6 mm
filler blocks

6 mm grooves
6 mm deep

6 mm

76 mm

B

A

C

D

100 mm

89 mm

A

114 mm

Thumb-grasp

E

6 mm

6 mm

6 mm

25 mm brad

112 mm

216 mm

6 mm grooves
6 mm deep

16 mm

3 mm

THUMB-GRASP DETAIL

APPLYING AN ANTIQUE, PAINTED FINISH TO THE BOX

16 Sand the box and lid. To give the candle box the antique painted look shown by the candle box in the photograph, the unpainted surface must be distressed first. Follow the technique for distressing furniture described in the punched-tin pie safe project (see page 75).

17 Apply the finish in layers. The process described below yields great results but also requires patience, as seven coats of finishes are applied. Start by wiping on a walnut stain. After the stain has dried, apply two protective layers of a clear finish (preferably polyurethane) and lightly sand the second coat before laying down a primer paint. Chose a primer that is close in colour to one popular in colonial times, such as iron-oxide red (used here), black or mustard yellow.

18 When the primer has dried completely, apply soldier blue paint as a colour coat. You can use either a latex or an oil-based paint and you can apply one over the other. However, if you use an oil-based paint as a first coat, sand it before applying a latex finish over it. Otherwise, the latex material may pool or not adhere properly.

19 Using sand paper, wear away the colour coat along edges, corners and other areas where the paint would have worn off through use. Then, referring to the Step 19 illustration (see below), use a 320-grit paper to lightly sand the entire surface. Sand down to the primer coat around worn areas. The two layers of polyurethane you applied will protect the stained wood if you accidentally sand through the primer. Try not to reveal the bare wood, however, as the stained wood will resemble old wood more closely.

20 Referring to the Step 20 illustration (see below left), apply a coat of mahogany, oil-based gel stain over the surface, then wipe away the majority of it with a lint-free cloth. Leave some gel stain deposits in crevices and other areas not likely to have received wear and cleaning over the years. The residue left behind after you have removed the stain will simulate the buildup of grime, referred to as a 'patina'.

21 Add a bit more character to the candle box by spattering the surface. To achieve this accent, refer to the description of the procedure in the punched-tin pie safe project (see steps 31 and 32 on page 75). In addition to the mahogany oil-based stain gel used to simulate a patina, you will require mineral turpentine to create these speckles.

STEP 19 Use sandpaper to remove the colour coat without sanding through the primer.

STEP 20 To simulate patina, apply a mahogany gel stain to the nooks and crannies.

Garden Trug

This long, narrow, wooden basket, known as a garden 'trug', is handy for carrying flowers and fruit from the garden to the house. Finished in a bright, natural colour, it also makes a superb planter box.

ASSEMBLING THE TRUG

1 Cut two pieces of 240 x 19 mm treated pine, 450 mm long for the ends (A). Enlarge the End Pattern (see page 109) and transfer the shape to the end pieces. Cut just outside the line with a jigsaw and sand to the line to obtain the final shape for each piece. Cut the bottom edge to 15 degrees so that the ends will turn outwards. On the inside of the end pieces, mark the positions of the holes for the handle (see the End Pattern, page 109).

2 Clamp an end face up on a workbench above a piece of scrap timber. Install a 22 mm Forstner bit in a drill and, using a sliding bevel set at 15 degrees as a guide, drill the handle hole. Repeat the procedure for the other end.

3 Cut two pieces of 140 x 19 mm treated pine, 660 mm long for the sides (B). With a marking gauge set at 4 mm, score a line along one face of each side, parallel to the edge.

4 Clamp one side in a vice and use a smoothing plane to plane the edges at a 15-degree angle, until the outside edge meets the scored line. Repeat the procedure for the other side. Then, using a sliding bevel set at 15-degrees, mark sloped ends on each side piece, from the top edge back to the bevelled edge. Cut along the lines with a jigsaw.

5 On each sloped end of the trug sides, draw a parallel line 20 mm in from the end. Place a mark 25 mm in from each edge along this line and a mark midway between the two marks. Using a 4.5 mm bit, drill clearance holes at each of these marks, and then countersink the holes on the outside face.

6 Secure the ends 10 mm in from the sides with adhesive and 6 g x 30 mm screws. Remove excess adhesive with a wet rag.

7 Cut the base (C) from 215 x 19 mm pine, 600 mm long. On the face, mark a line 4 mm in along each end and edge. Mark another line all the way around the edges 10 mm up.

8 Using a hand plane, plane a bevel off the corner, joining these lines. (It is a good idea to plane the end grain first to prevent chipping.)

9 Sit the top part onto the base, making sure it is parallel and centred (the sides should be 10 mm in from the edges of the base, the ends 6 mm in). Draw a line along the inside and outside of the sides, onto the base. Remove the top assembly and mark the positions for three screws midway between the two lines.

10 Drill clearance holes through the base using a 4.5 mm drill bit, at the same angle as the side. Countersink from the bottom. Apply adhesive to the bottom edge of the sides and ends, then sit them on the base, using the marks as a guide. To screw the pieces together, slide one end of the trug off the bench and insert the 30 mm screws from the bottom.

FINISHING

11 Slide the dowel handle into the ends from one end. Apply a little adhesive to the part of the dowel which will be in the hole, and rotate it into position. Fill any holes with filler, and sand the trug with 120- then 180-grit paper (either by hand or with orbital sander). Apply a finish of your choice.

The thin carrier and handle sections of the trug are formed by planing or resawing timber pieces to the correct size.

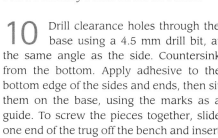

TIMBER

FINISHED SIZE IN MM

PART	W	T	L	MATERIAL	QUANTITY
A ends	240	19	450	TP	2
B sides	140	19	660	TP	2
C base	215	19	600	TP	1

Material key: TP = treated pine

OTHER MATERIALS

- 850 mm length of 22 mm treated pine dowel
- PVA adhesive
- 8 g x 30 mm screws
- Paint or lacquer; 120-, 180-grit sandpaper

TOOLS

- Portable electric drill
- Drill bits: 2.5 mm, 4.5 mm, countersink, 22 mm Forstner
- Jigsaw
- Mitre drop saw
- Smoothing or hand plane
- Tape measure
- Fold-out rule or 300 mm steel rule
- Sliding bevel
- Square
- Compass
- Phillips head screwdriver or drill bit
- Orbital sander
- Cork sanding block
- G-cramp

Substitute other tools or equipment as desired. Additional common hand tools and clamps may be required.

Always observe the safety precautions in the owner's manual when using a tool or a piece of machinery.

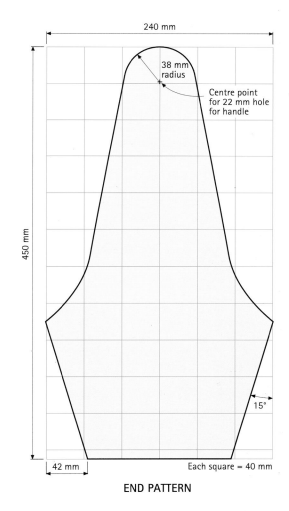

850 mm

Dowel handle

10 mm

6 mm

600 mm

660 mm

FRONT VIEW

B

A

C

A

B

TOP VIEW

A

C

215 mm

END VIEW

240 mm

38 mm radius

Centre point for 22 mm hole for handle

450 mm

15°

42 mm

Each square = 40 mm

END PATTERN

Glossary

auxiliary fence used to support timber at its cutting point

bar clamp adaptation of G-clamp; self-locking arm is adjusted quickly by sliding it along a serrated bar until the adjustment is made with a screw; jaw sizes range from 150 mm to 1000 mm with a throat depth of from 80 mm to 120 mm

bradawl thin, steel shaft with one end flattened and sharpened and the other fixed into a wooden handle; when the cutting edge is placed across the grain and forced into the timber, it cuts a hole for a small wood screw

chamfer corner planed off at an angle of forty-five degrees

cleat strip of timber fixed across a second piece

counterbore cut a hole that permits the head of a screw or bolt to lie below the surface of the timber

countersink concave boring in wood to receive a screw head so the surface of the screw is lower than that of the wood

countersink bit makes a tapered recess for a countersunk woodscrew; drill pilot and clearance holes first to centre the point of the countersink bit, then run the drill at a fast speed for a clean finish

crosscut saw across the grain

dado saws set of saws used for cutting trenches and rebates

dowel pin of wood for use in joined timber constructions

dowel bit used for boring dowel holes and drilling out waste for mortises; smaller sizes of twist drill can be used for screw holes and general cabinet work

dowel centre used to mark the centre of a hole for a dowel joint

dowel jig used as an aid when drilling dowel holes

drill-and-counterbore bit performs like drill-and-countersink but also drills a neat counterbored hole that can be filled with a wooden plug to hide the screw head

drill-and-countersink bit drills a pilot hole, shank clearance hole and countersink hole in one operation; size varies to match common wood screws

drum sander small, round piece of timber covered with sandpaper used to smooth and clean up timber

featherboard piece of timber with saw cuts forming 'feathers' on one end that acts as a guard

fence adjustable guide that keeps the cutting edge of a tool a set distance from the edge of a workpiece

filigree decorated wooden panel used in furniture

flush level with or even with the surrounding surfaces

Forstner bit drill bit of superior quality that leaves clean holes with flat bottoms; bits with diameters up to 50 mm are available; not deflected by knots or wood grain, and easily bores overlapping holes and holes that run out to the edge of the work; Forstner bits must be run at a slow speed

jointer surface planing machine

kerf width of the saw cut

kickback action of a power tool when it jumps backwards or throws material backwards as a result of its blade or its cutter jamming

mitre gauge or crosscut fence gauge used on a table saw for crosscutting at various angles

mortise and tenon common joint used in furniture joinery

pilot hole small hole sized to suit the screw thread

plug cutter driven into the side grain of timber to cut a cylindrical plug to match the hole left by a drill-and-counterbore bit

rebate stepped recess along the edge of a workpiece, usually as part of a joint

rip saw along the grain

rounding-over cutter produces a simple radiused edge or, when set lower, cuts an ovolo bead (radiused edge with a stepped shoulder or quick)

sash cramp used for holding parts together while gluing; ranges in size from 600 mm to 2000 mm; consists of T-section bar with two adjustable shoes that can be repositioned and a cramping screw

shank hole hole drilled into timber to enable the shank of a screw to fit inside

slip feather spline piece of timber inserted across a joint to add strength

spring clamps used for fast application when holding small work

square components at right angles to each other

stretcher rail horizontal frame member

table saw multipurpose crosscut and ripping saw

toggle bolt used on plaster-board ceilings and walls, with wings that open automatically when inserted through a hole, spreading the load of the fixture over the surface

trammel points used like an oversized compass for marking large curves

trench groove cut across timber grain

utility knife available in various shapes, most commonly the Stanley knife with its removable blade

web or band cramps used for applying pressure in areas unsuited to normal clamping procedures

Index

Published by Murdoch Books® a division of Murdoch Magazines Pty Ltd,
GPO Box 1203, Sydney NSW 1045.

Managing Editor, Craft and Gardening: Christine Eslick
Editor: Catherine Magoffin
Designer: Michèle Lichtenberger
Illustrator: Stephen Pollitt
Photography: *Better Homes and Gardens® Picture Library

CEO and Publisher: Anne Wilson

National Library of Australia Cataloguing-in-Publication Data
Woodworking projects country-style.
Includes index. ISBN 0 86411 973 9.
1. Woodwork – Amateurs' manuals. I. Title: Better homes and gardens.
684.08

Printed by Prestige Litho, Queensland
PRINTED IN AUSTRALIA

First published 2000
Australian distribution to supermarkets and newsagents by Gordon & Gotch Ltd,
68 Kingsgrove Road, Belmore NSW 2192.
Distributed in NZ by Golden Press, a division of HarperCollins Publishers,
31 View Road, Glenfield, PO Box 1, Auckland 1.

*Better Homes and Gardens® (Trade Mark) Regd TM of Meredith Corporation